# DOOM: THE DARK AGES GAME GUIDE

# CHAPTER 1: INTRODUCTION

## 1.1    Welcome to DOOM: The Dark Ages

Welcome to DOOM: The Dark Ages, a dark and thrilling entry into the legendary DOOM franchise. In this unique twist on the series, players are transported to a medieval world steeped in ancient magic, dark creatures, and gothic architecture. Unlike its futuristic predecessors, DOOM: The Dark Ages introduces a mix of traditional DOOM combat with medieval weaponry and eerie, atmospheric levels.

Setting the Stage:
The game takes place in a time where humanity is on the brink of collapse. Mysterious dark forces have summoned powerful, otherworldly entities into the world, threatening to obliterate any hope of survival. As the protagonist, you play a lone warrior known only as the Slayer, tasked with eliminating the demonic forces that ravage the land. Your mission: To battle through treacherous forests, ancient castles, cryptic ruins, and dark catacombs to save humanity from utter annihilation.

Key Features of DOOM: The Dark Ages:

- Medieval Combat with a DOOM Twist: Wield a variety of melee weapons such as swords, axes, and enchanted maces, along with traditional firearms to defeat the evil forces.
- Atmospheric World: The setting combines dark fantasy and gothic architecture, featuring haunted forests, decaying castles, and other eerie environments.

- Powerful Enemies: Face off against unique demonic creatures inspired by medieval lore, including undead knights, hellish beasts, and eldritch horrors.
- Challenging Gameplay: As with any DOOM game, expect fast-paced combat, intense action, and complex level design that requires both precision and strategy.

## 1.2 Game Overview & Storyline

DOOM: The Dark Ages brings the iconic franchise into a hauntingly medieval world, blending the fast-paced, intense action of the DOOM series with the dark, mystic elements of ancient fantasy. This game marks a dramatic departure from the science-fiction setting of previous DOOM titles and introduces a gothic, hellish universe where ancient magic and nightmarish beasts collide.

*Game Overview*

In DOOM: The Dark Ages, players take on the role of the Slayer, a legendary warrior chosen by a mysterious order to battle against the dark forces that have overrun the land. The game features a rich blend of medieval combat and DOOM's signature fast-paced action, with a wide variety of weapons, spells, and enemies to engage with.

Key Features:

- Combat Mechanics: A mix of classic DOOM-style gunplay with powerful medieval weaponry such as swords, crossbows, and enchanted maces. In addition, magical abilities can be used to unleash devastating attacks or provide powerful buffs.
- Demonic Enemies: The game introduces a wide range of creatures from medieval myth and legend, including undead

knights, demonic sorcerers, spectral beasts, and horrors from other dimensions.

- Environmental Design: The levels are meticulously crafted to reflect the ominous medieval aesthetic, from haunted castles and decaying villages to ancient crypts and dark forests teeming with hidden dangers.
- Exploration: Players will navigate large, complex levels filled with secrets, hidden passages, and side objectives that encourage thorough exploration and discovery.

*Storyline*

The world of DOOM: The Dark Ages is a land on the brink of destruction. Centuries of peace were shattered when an ancient artifact, known as the Demon's Sigil, was uncovered by a secretive group of sorcerers. In their greed and arrogance, the sorcerers sought to harness its immense power, only to unleash a dark force that shattered the barriers between worlds.

This malevolent power tore through the land, summoning twisted demonic creatures and unleashing an era of nightmares. Villages were abandoned, kingdoms fell, and mankind was pushed to the edge of extinction. However, in the darkest hour, the Order of the Slayer, a group of ancient knights dedicated to protecting humanity, chose their last hope: a lone warrior, the Slayer, to combat the rising threat.

With an indomitable will and unmatched strength, the Slayer embarks on a journey to confront the demonic forces, battle through corrupted lands, and ultimately destroy the Demon's Sigil before it can plunge the world into eternal darkness.

As the Slayer, you'll travel across several regions:

- The Forsaken Forests: Haunted woodlands filled with twisted creatures and dark magic.

- Cursed Castles: Desolate, ruined fortresses where the most powerful enemies reside.
- The Abyssal Depths: Underground catacombs and hellish caverns teeming with demonic spawn.
- The Heart of Darkness: The final battleground where the Demon's Sigil resides, guarded by an army of ancient evil forces.

Along the way, you will uncover hidden secrets, ancient lore, and clues that lead to the ultimate showdown with the Demon's Sigil and the dark sorcerers who unleashed it.

Themes:

- Fate of Humanity: The game explores humanity's last chance to survive as the world collapses under the weight of dark magic and demonic forces.
- Power and Corruption: A recurring theme in the game is the corrupting influence of power, as seen in the sorcerers' greed and the twisted evolution of demonic creatures.
- The Hero's Journey: Players will guide the Slayer through personal and epic battles, ultimately confronting the ancient evil in an epic, final confrontation.

## 1.3   Basic Gameplay Mechanics

In DOOM: The Dark Ages, the gameplay combines the signature fast-paced combat of the DOOM franchise with medieval fantasy elements, resulting in a dynamic and engaging experience. The mechanics are designed to offer both familiarity for long-time DOOM fans and fresh challenges for newcomers. From the frantic action to the strategic use of weapons and magic, here's an overview of the core gameplay mechanics.

### 1.3.1 Core Gameplay Loop

At its heart, DOOM: The Dark Ages follows the core loop that fans of the series know and love: explore, fight, and upgrade. Each level challenges players with new enemies, environments, and obstacles to overcome, all while progressing through a story-driven campaign.

The gameplay focuses heavily on action with constant movement, strategic combat, and rapid decision-making. You'll need to react quickly to enemy ambushes, explore each level for hidden items and secrets, and constantly upgrade your arsenal to survive the growing threat of the dark forces.

### 1.3.2 Combat System

DOOM: The Dark Ages integrates a mix of medieval weapons, ranged firearms, and powerful magical abilities into its combat system. Here's how each element works:

- Melee Combat:
  The game introduces a variety of melee weapons, such as:
    - Swords: Balanced in speed and damage, ideal for close-range combat against multiple enemies.
    - Axes: Slower but capable of inflicting heavier damage to tough enemies.
    - Maces: Used for dealing damage in wide arcs, effective against crowds of weaker enemies.
    - Greatswords and Spears: Powerful two-handed weapons for heavy damage, but leave the player vulnerable to enemy attacks if used recklessly.

  Melee attacks also have a stamina meter: using heavy weapons or performing combo moves will drain stamina, forcing you to manage your attacks carefully.

- Ranged Combat:
  Ranged weapons include traditional firearms and crossbows, such as:
    o Crossbow: Fires bolts that deal moderate damage but have a slow rate of fire. Useful for picking off enemies from a distance.
    o Firearm (Pistol/Shotgun): A range of gunplay that offers fast, powerful shots for dealing with foes at mid-to-close range.
    o Magical Firearms: A blend of crossbow and magic, these weapons can fire elemental projectiles like fireballs or ice bolts.
- Magical Abilities:
  As the Slayer, you have access to powerful spells that allow you to manipulate the battlefield:
    o Fireball: Launches a fiery orb that explodes on impact.
    o Frostbolt: Freezes enemies in place, giving you a brief moment to attack or escape.
    o Heal: Restores a portion of your health but consumes mana. Mana regenerates over time, but faster when you slay enemies.
    o Shield of Light: Temporarily increases your defense against enemy attacks, providing a tactical advantage when overwhelmed.

To use magic, you must manage your mana pool, which regenerates slowly but can be replenished by finding magical runes or defeating specific enemies.

### 1.3.3 Movement & Exploration

Movement is fast and fluid, allowing the Slayer to navigate the gothic world with ease. The game encourages constant mobility, as enemies often surround you or attack from multiple angles. Here are the key movement mechanics:

- Running & Dodging:
  The Slayer has a quick sprint ability that helps escape danger or close the distance with enemies. You can also dodge incoming attacks by quickly moving sideways or rolling.
- Jumping & Climbing:
  Verticality plays an important role in DOOM: The Dark Ages, with platforms, ledges, and obstacles that require precise jumping and climbing. Players can leap across gaps, climb walls, and access hidden areas by navigating these elements.
- Interactive Environments:
  Many levels contain traps, levers, and mechanisms that need to be activated to progress. Players may encounter locked doors, puzzles requiring hidden switches, or environmental hazards that need to be bypassed. Exploration is key to uncovering secrets and finding hidden upgrades.

*1.3.4 Health & Armor*

In DOOM: The Dark Ages, health and armor are the foundation of your survival.

- Health:
  The Slayer has a health pool that is depleted when taking damage from enemies. Health can be replenished by picking up Health Potions scattered throughout levels or by finding healing altars hidden in certain locations. However, certain magical enemies can also drain health over time, adding a layer of complexity to encounters.
- Armor:
  Armor helps mitigate damage and acts as a buffer between the Slayer and enemy attacks. Players can find armor shards and plates to repair or upgrade their armor during gameplay. Upgrading armor increases its durability, giving you more time in combat before your health begins to deplete.

### 1.3.5 Weapon Upgrades & Customization

Weapons in DOOM: The Dark Ages are not static; they can be upgraded and customized through a variety of in-game systems:

- Weapon Mods:
  Some weapons can be enhanced with special mods, such as explosive projectiles, rapid-fire enhancements, or elemental damage. Mods are often found in secret areas, awarded for completing side quests, or dropped by powerful enemies.
- Enchantments:
  Magic-infused weapons can be enchanted with spells, adding effects like poison, flame, or freezing to your attacks. These enchantments make weapons more effective against specific types of enemies.
- Upgrade Stations:
  Special upgrade stations allow you to enhance your equipment using a resource called Essence, which is gained from defeating major enemies or completing level objectives.

### 1.3.6 Enemy AI & Behavior

Enemies in DOOM: The Dark Ages are not simply mindless creatures; they are tactical and react to your movements. For example:

- Ranged enemies will keep their distance and shoot projectiles at you, forcing you to dodge and return fire.
- Melee enemies will charge toward you, trying to overwhelm you with sheer numbers.
- Spellcasting enemies may use debuffs, curses, or environmental manipulation to turn the tide of battle against you.

Different types of enemies exhibit unique behavior patterns, requiring players to adjust their tactics in combat. Some demons may focus on summoning additional enemies, while others might teleport around the battlefield, making them harder to target.

### 1.3.7 Progression & Difficulty

As you progress through the game, the difficulty naturally increases. More enemies, tougher bosses, and intricate puzzles will test your abilities. However, DOOM: The Dark Ages offers a dynamic difficulty system that adapts to your performance:

- If you are struggling, the game will make slight adjustments to make it easier (e.g., more health pickups or less aggressive enemies).
- If you're breezing through the game, it will increase the intensity, adding more challenges and powerful enemies.

Skill Trees & Unlockables:
As you defeat enemies and complete levels, you earn experience points, which can be spent to unlock new abilities or weapon enhancements. Players can customize the Slayer's skills to suit their playstyle, whether you prefer devastating magic, improved weapon combat, or enhanced mobility.

# CHAPTER 2: GETTING STARTED

## 2.1 Installing DOOM: The Dark Ages

Before diving into the action, it's essential to get DOOM: The Dark Ages properly installed on your system. Whether you're playing on PC, console, or another platform, the installation process will vary slightly depending on your chosen system. Below, we provide step-by-step instructions to ensure you can get started quickly.

### 2.1.1 System Requirements

Before installing, it's important to check that your system meets the minimum or recommended requirements to ensure smooth gameplay. These requirements can vary slightly depending on the platform, but here are the general specs for PC players:

Minimum System Requirements:

- OS: Windows 10 (64-bit) or macOS Mojave or higher
- Processor: Intel Core i5 or AMD Ryzen 5
- Memory: 8 GB RAM
- Graphics: NVIDIA GTX 1060 or AMD RX 580 (or equivalent)
- DirectX: Version 12
- Storage: 50 GB free space
- Sound: DirectX compatible

Recommended System Requirements:

- OS: Windows 10 (64-bit) or macOS Catalina or higher
- Processor: Intel Core i7 or AMD Ryzen 7
- Memory: 16 GB RAM

- Graphics: NVIDIA RTX 2070 or AMD RX 6800 (or equivalent)
- Storage: 50 GB SSD (or faster)
- Sound: DirectX compatible or high-definition audio card

### 2.1.2 Installing on PC (Steam/Official Website)

If you're playing DOOM: The Dark Ages on PC, the game is available through both Steam and the official DOOM website. Follow the steps below for each method:

Using Steam:

1. Download and Install Steam:
   - If you don't have Steam installed, visit Steam's website and download the client for your system.
   - Install Steam and log in with your account (or create a new account if you don't have one).
2. Search for DOOM: The Dark Ages:
   - Open Steam and go to the search bar at the top right of the Steam client.
   - Type in "DOOM: The Dark Ages" and press Enter.
3. Purchase the Game:
   - On the game's page, click the "Add to Cart" button and proceed to checkout.
   - After completing the purchase, the game will be added to your Library.
4. Download and Install:
   - Go to your Library and find DOOM: The Dark Ages.
   - Click on the game's name, then click Install.
   - Choose a download location and start the installation process. The game will automatically download and install.
5. Launch the Game:
   - Once the game is installed, click the "Play" button in your Steam Library to launch DOOM: The Dark Ages.

Using the Official Website:

1. Visit the Official Website:
   - Go to the official DOOM: The Dark Ages website, where you can purchase and download the game. You may need to create a new account or log in.
2. Download the Installer:
   - Once purchased, you'll be able to download the game installer specific to your operating system (Windows or macOS).
3. Run the Installer:
   - After downloading, open the installer file and follow the on-screen instructions. The game will be installed on your selected drive.
4. Launch the Game:
   - After installation, navigate to the game's shortcut on your desktop (or in the Start menu) and launch DOOM: The Dark Ages.

*2.1.3 Installing on Consoles (PlayStation, Xbox)*

If you're installing DOOM: The Dark Ages on a console, the process is streamlined through each platform's digital store.

PlayStation (PS4/PS5):

1. Go to the PlayStation Store:
   - Turn on your console and navigate to the PlayStation Store on the main menu.
2. Search for DOOM: The Dark Ages:
   - In the search bar, type "DOOM: The Dark Ages" and select the game from the results.
3. Purchase and Download:
   - Click "Add to Cart" and proceed with the payment. Once the transaction is complete, the game will begin downloading automatically.

4. Play the Game:
   o   After downloading, the game will appear on your home
       screen. Select the game icon to start playing.

Xbox (Xbox One/Series X|S):

1. Go to the Microsoft Store:
   o   On your Xbox, press the Xbox button to open the menu
       and navigate to the Microsoft Store.
2. Search for DOOM: The Dark Ages:
   o   Type "DOOM: The Dark Ages" into the search bar and
       select the game.
3. Purchase and Download:
   o   Select Buy and complete the purchase. The game will
       begin downloading immediately after payment.
4. Launch the Game:
   o   Once installed, the game will appear on your Home
       screen. Select it to start playing.

*2.1.4 Installing on Other Platforms (Switch, PC VR)*

For Nintendo Switch and PC VR players, installation follows similar
digital store procedures:

Nintendo Switch:

1. Go to the Nintendo eShop:
   o   From the Home menu, select the eShop icon and
       search for DOOM: The Dark Ages.
2. Download and Install:
   o   Purchase and download the game directly from the
       eShop. The game will install automatically after the
       purchase.
3. Start Playing:
   o   Once downloaded, the game icon will appear on the
       Home screen. Select it to begin playing.

PC VR (Oculus Rift/SteamVR):

1. Open Oculus Store or SteamVR:
   o Launch either the Oculus Store (for Oculus headsets) or Steam (for SteamVR headsets).
2. Search for DOOM: The Dark Ages:
   o Use the search bar to find DOOM: The Dark Ages.
3. Purchase and Install:
   o Once you've purchased the game, it will begin downloading automatically.
4. Launch the Game:
   o After installation, launch the game from your Library and adjust your VR settings for optimal experience.

*2.1.5 Troubleshooting Installation Issues*

If you encounter any issues during installation, here are some tips to resolve them:

- Check System Requirements: Ensure your device meets the minimum system requirements to run the game.
- Ensure Sufficient Storage Space: Confirm that you have enough free space on your hard drive or SSD to download the game.
- Reboot Your System: If the game isn't installing properly, restart your console or PC and try again.
- Update Your Software: Make sure your operating system, gaming platform, and graphics drivers are up-to-date.
- Verify Game Files (Steam): If you're on PC and using Steam, right-click on DOOM: The Dark Ages in your Library, go to Properties, and verify the integrity of the game files.

## 2.2 Game Setup & Configuration

After installing DOOM: The Dark Ages, the next step is to ensure the game is properly set up and configured for the best experience. Whether you're playing on PC, console, or VR, customizing the game's settings will help optimize performance, enhance visuals, and tailor gameplay to your preferences. This chapter covers everything you need to know to get your game ready to go!

*2.2.1 General Settings*

Upon launching DOOM: The Dark Ages for the first time, you'll be greeted with the Main Menu, where you can access various settings, including game options, video, audio, and control configurations.

To adjust the settings, navigate to the Options menu from the Main Menu, where you'll find the following categories:

*2.2.2 Video Settings*

The video settings allow you to customize the visual quality of the game, ensuring smooth performance based on your system capabilities. Here's a breakdown of the key video settings:

- Resolution:
    - Choose the resolution that suits your display. The game supports a range of resolutions from 720p to 4K (if supported by your system).
    - PC: Typically set to the native resolution of your monitor.
    - Consoles: Set automatically based on your TV or monitor resolution.
- Graphics Quality:

- o Low / Medium / High / Ultra: Depending on your system, you can choose the graphics quality that balances performance and visual fidelity.
    - Low: Best for low-end systems or when you want smoother performance over visuals.
    - Ultra: Best for high-end systems for maximum visual detail, including advanced lighting, textures, and environmental effects.
- Anti-Aliasing:
    - o Enables smoother edges and improved image quality. Turn this setting on for better visual clarity, especially at higher resolutions.
    - o Options include FXAA, TAA, or Off, with TAA providing the highest quality but at the cost of performance.
- V-Sync:
    - o Enable this to synchronize the frame rate with your monitor's refresh rate, reducing screen tearing.
    - o Disable it if you prefer a higher frame rate but are okay with occasional tearing.
- Field of View (FOV):
    - o Adjusts how much of the game world you can see. Higher FOV values give you a wider perspective, ideal for combat and exploration.
    - o Recommended to set around 90-100 for a balanced experience.
- Motion Blur:
    - o This effect simulates the blurring of fast-moving objects. You can disable this if it causes discomfort or if you prefer sharper visuals.
- Frame Rate Cap:
    - o Set a cap for the game's frame rate. Disabling the cap will allow the game to run at the maximum FPS supported by your system.
    - o You can choose specific frame rate caps, such as 30 FPS, 60 FPS, or Uncapped.

### 2.2.3 Audio Settings

Sound plays a significant role in creating atmosphere, and the audio settings allow you to tweak the game's sound for optimal immersion. Here's how you can adjust the audio options:

- Master Volume:
  - Controls the overall game sound volume. Adjust this to a level that's comfortable for you.
- Music Volume:
  - Adjust the volume of the game's background music. You can lower it if you prefer more immersive environmental sounds.
- SFX Volume:
  - Controls the volume of in-game sound effects, including combat noises, enemy growls, weapon sounds, and environmental effects.
- Dialogue Volume:
  - Controls the volume of in-game voice acting, important during cutscenes and interactions.
- Subtitles:
  - You can enable or disable subtitles for dialogue, helping you follow along with the story, especially in action-heavy sections.
- Audio Output:
  - Choose between Stereo, 5.1 Surround, or 7.1 Surround sound for the best experience, depending on your audio hardware.

### 2.2.4 Control Settings

The controls are crucial for smooth gameplay, so configuring them to your preference will improve your gaming experience. Here's how you can adjust the controls:

- Control Layout:

- o Choose between Default, Legacy, or Custom control schemes.
    - Default: The recommended control setup for most players.
    - Legacy: A setup based on older DOOM titles, for players who prefer a more classic control style.
    - Custom: Allows you to remap buttons for a personalized layout.
- Mouse & Keyboard (PC):
    - o Mouse Sensitivity: Adjust the sensitivity for precise aiming. Increase sensitivity for faster movement, or decrease it for more control.
    - o Invert Mouse: Enable this option if you prefer to invert the mouse movement (up/down axis).
- Gamepad (PC, Consoles):
    - o Controller Vibration: Toggle controller vibration to enhance immersion.
    - o Button Mapping: Customize button layouts for controllers, allowing you to remap actions to preferred buttons.
- Look Sensitivity (PC, Console):
    - o Adjust the speed of camera movement when using the mouse or controller right stick. Higher values result in quicker turns, while lower values offer more precision.
- Auto-Aim (Console):
    - o Enable or disable auto-aim, which helps target enemies more effectively. This setting is primarily useful for console players but can be adjusted for difficulty.

*2.2.5 Game Difficulty Settings*

Adjusting the game's difficulty ensures that players of all skill levels can enjoy DOOM: The Dark Ages. The available difficulty settings are:

- Easy: A more forgiving experience, with weaker enemies and more health pickups. Ideal for newcomers or players seeking a casual experience.
- Normal: The standard difficulty, providing a balanced challenge with fair enemy strength and health.
- Hard: A more challenging experience, where enemies are tougher, and resources are scarcer. Recommended for experienced players seeking a tougher challenge.
- Nightmare: The ultimate challenge, with extremely aggressive enemies, limited resources, and heightened difficulty. Only the most skilled players should attempt this difficulty.

You can adjust the difficulty at any time from the Options menu to match your skill level or desired challenge.

*2.2.6 Accessibility Options*

To ensure DOOM: The Dark Ages is accessible to all players, there are various accessibility settings that can be customized to suit different needs:

- Colorblind Mode:
    - Adjust the color scheme to assist players with color vision impairments. You can toggle between several modes (e.g., Deuteranopia, Protanopia).
- Subtitles:
    - Enable subtitles for all dialogue, even in action-packed sections, to ensure players don't miss any critical information.
- Audio Cues:
    - Enable visual cues for key audio events (e.g., enemy growls, explosions) to aid hearing-impaired players.
- Motion Sensitivity:
    - Reduce or eliminate camera shake and motion blur effects, which may be helpful for players sensitive to motion sickness.

- Button Hold Toggle:
  - Instead of holding buttons for certain actions (e.g., sprinting, crouching), you can toggle them on/off with a single press.

### 2.2.7 Save & Load Settings

DOOM: The Dark Ages provides the flexibility to save and load your progress at any point during the game:

- Auto-Save:
  - The game will automatically save your progress at key moments (e.g., after defeating a boss or reaching a checkpoint).
- Manual Saves:
  - You can manually save your progress by selecting Save Game in the Pause Menu. It's recommended to save before major encounters to avoid losing progress.
- Load Game:
  - If you wish to load a previous save, go to the Load Game section from the Main Menu to choose the saved file you wish to continue from.

### 2.2.8 Finalizing Setup

Once you've configured all your settings to your liking, you can exit the Options menu. Make sure to apply any changes before returning to the main game. You're now ready to embark on your journey through the dark medieval world of DOOM: The Dark Ages!

## 2.3 Controls and Interface

Understanding the controls and the interface is crucial for navigating DOOM: The Dark Ages effectively. This chapter will cover the controls for PC, consoles, and VR setups, as well as a detailed breakdown of the game's interface, so you can focus on the action without any distractions.

*2.3.1 Control Scheme Overview*

DOOM: The Dark Ages offers several control options depending on the platform. Below is an overview of the standard control layouts for each platform, along with customizable options to match your preferences.

## 2.3.2 PC Controls (Mouse & Keyboard)

For PC players, the mouse and keyboard provide precision and quick reactions. Here's the default control scheme for DOOM: The Dark Ages:

- W, A, S, D: Move character forward, left, backward, and right, respectively.
- Mouse Movement: Look around and aim. Mouse sensitivity can be adjusted in the settings.
- Left Mouse Button (LMB): Fire primary weapon.
- Right Mouse Button (RMB): Use secondary weapon or alternative fire mode (varies per weapon).
- Spacebar: Jump.
- Ctrl (Hold): Crouch.
- Shift: Sprint (Hold).
- R: Reload weapon.
- E: Interact (e.g., picking up items, opening doors).
- Q: Use item (health pack, power-ups).
- F: Melee attack.
- 1-5 (Number Keys): Switch between weapons.
- Tab: Open inventory (if applicable) or mission objectives.
- M: Open map (if available).
- Esc: Pause menu (for settings, save/load, etc.).
- T: Toggle flashlight (if the game has a flashlight mechanic).

### 2.3.3 Console Controls (PlayStation / Xbox)

For PlayStation and Xbox players, the controls are optimized for controllers, providing a more intuitive and immersive experience. Below is a breakdown of the control schemes:

*PlayStation (PS4/PS5)*

- Left Stick: Move character.
- Right Stick: Look around and aim.
- R2: Fire primary weapon.
- L2: Aim down sights (if applicable) or alternative fire mode.
- X: Jump.
- Circle: Crouch.
- Square: Melee attack.
- R1: Sprint (Hold).
- L1: Use item (e.g., health packs).
- Options Button: Pause menu.
- Touchpad: Toggle map (if available) or in-game interface.
- D-Pad Up: Select weapon.
- D-Pad Right/Left: Use quick item (e.g., power-ups).
- R3 (Click): Toggle flashlight.

*Xbox (Xbox One/Series X|S)*

- Left Stick: Move character.
- Right Stick: Look around and aim.
- RT: Fire primary weapon.
- LT: Aim down sights (if applicable) or alternative fire mode.
- A: Jump.
- B: Crouch.
- X: Melee attack.
- RB: Sprint (Hold).
- LB: Use item (e.g., health packs).
- Start Button: Pause menu.
- Select Button: Toggle map or in-game interface.

- D-Pad Up: Select weapon.
- D-Pad Right/Left: Use quick item (e.g., power-ups).
- RS (Click): Toggle flashlight.

## 2.3.4 VR Controls (PC VR - Oculus Rift / SteamVR)

For VR players, DOOM: The Dark Ages provides an immersive experience where physical movement and gestures play a key role. Here's a breakdown of VR controls for Oculus Rift and SteamVR:

- Left Thumbstick: Move character.
- Right Thumbstick: Look around and aim.
- Left Trigger: Melee attack.
- Right Trigger: Fire primary weapon.
- Left Grip: Interact with objects (e.g., picking up items, opening doors).
- Right Grip: Use secondary weapon or alternative fire mode.
- A/B (Oculus) / X/Y (SteamVR): Jump.
- Menu Button: Open the in-game interface or pause menu.
- Touchpad or Joystick on the Controller: Sprint or dash (hold).
- Head Tracking: Move your head to change the view and look around your environment. Headset tracking is critical for aiming and engaging enemies.

### 2.3.5 The Game Interface

The interface in DOOM: The Dark Ages is designed for quick access to key information while keeping your attention on the action. Here's an overview of the main elements of the game interface.

## 2.3.6 HUD (Heads-Up Display)

The HUD provides critical information to the player during gameplay:

- Health Bar: Located at the top-left corner, indicating your character's health. It's color-coded (typically green) and will deplete as you take damage.
- Armor: Represented as a blue bar near the health bar. Armor absorbs damage, reducing the impact on your health.
- Ammunition: Shows the current ammo count for your selected weapon. This is usually displayed near the bottom-center or near the weapon icon.
- Weapon Icon: Displays the icon of the currently selected weapon along with the ammo count.
- Objective Indicator: A small icon or arrow indicating your current objective. This appears on the screen to guide you to your next task or mission.
- Radar / Mini-map: Located in the corner of the screen (typically bottom-right), showing a simplified layout of the area. Red dots typically represent enemies, and green dots show objectives or items.
- Power-ups/Items: Icons at the bottom or sides of the screen show what items or power-ups you currently have in your inventory (e.g., health packs, armor, special abilities).

## 2.3.7 Pause Menu

Accessed by pressing Esc (PC) or the Options button (PlayStation/Xbox), the Pause Menu allows you to manage your settings, save/load the game, and view additional information. The Pause Menu typically contains:

- Settings: Customize controls, video, audio, and gameplay options.
- Save/Load: Save your current progress or load a previous save.
- Mission Objectives: View your current objectives and progress.
- Map: View the area you are currently in, along with any undiscovered areas or key points of interest.
- Exit Game: Quit to the main menu or desktop.

### 2.3.8 Quick Items and Power-ups

During your journey, you'll encounter a variety of quick items and power-ups that can be accessed directly from your HUD or via hotkeys:

- Health Pack: Restores a portion of your health.
- Armor Pack: Restores or adds to your armor.
- Ammo Pack: Restores ammunition for your weapons.
- Special Power-ups: Temporary boosts (e.g., increased damage, invulnerability, speed boosts).
- Melee and Grenades: Melee attacks and explosive grenades (if applicable) are also accessible from quick-item slots.

### 2.3.9 Customization of Controls and Interface

You can customize the control layout and HUD to suit your preferences:

- Control Customization: If the default controls don't suit you, go into the options menu to remap your keys or buttons. You can also adjust sensitivity settings for both mouse and controller.
- HUD Customization: The game allows limited customization of the HUD, such as resizing certain elements (e.g., health, ammo) and enabling/disabling certain display features like the mini-map or objective indicators.

### 2.3.10 Advanced Tips for Mastering Controls

- Quick Weapon Switching: Learn the layout for quick weapon switching to react faster during combat. Use the number keys (PC) or D-pad (console) for quick access to the weapons you need.
- Strafe & Dodge: Use strafing (moving side-to-side) while shooting for better mobility during combat. On PC, use the A and D keys simultaneously with W and S for optimal

movement. On console, strafe with the Left Stick while shooting.

- Use the Map Effectively: If you're lost, use the map (M on PC or Touchpad on consoles) to quickly get back on track. The map can help you find objectives, enemies, or hidden items.

# CHAPTER 3: THE BASICS OF COMBAT

## 3.1 Weapons Overview

In DOOM: The Dark Ages, your survival depends on your arsenal. Whether you're up against swarms of enemies in tight corridors or facing giant, grotesque demons in open arenas, knowing which weapons to use and how to wield them will make all the difference. This chapter will break down the wide range of weapons available, categorizing them into ranged weapons and melee weapons, providing you with a comprehensive understanding of each weapon type

*3.1.1 Ranged Weapons*

Ranged weapons are your primary tools for taking down enemies from a distance. These weapons offer varying levels of power, accuracy, and firing rates. Here's a breakdown of the most essential ranged weapons in DOOM: The Dark Ages:

Crossbow

- Ammunition Type: Crossbow Bolts
- Firing Mode: Single shot, powerful but slow reload
- Range: Medium to long
- Description: A classic and reliable ranged weapon, the Crossbow allows you to hit enemies with precision from a distance. It's ideal for picking off enemies in the distance or hitting weak points. It's slower to reload, so use it carefully during intense combat situations.
    - Special Features:
        - Can be charged for a more powerful shot.

- Special crossbow bolts may be available, such as explosive or poisoned bolts.

## Bow & Arrow (Magical Variant)

- Ammunition Type: Magic Arrows
- Firing Mode: Single shot with arc or charged shot
- Range: Long-range, excellent for precision attacks
- Description: The Bow & Arrow in DOOM: The Dark Ages takes a more fantastical twist, with enchanted arrows capable of piercing through armor and causing elemental effects. This weapon is excellent for ranged attacks, especially against enemies with tough defenses.
  - Special Features:
    - Elemental Arrows: Arrows imbued with fire, ice, or lightning that cause additional status effects on enemies.
    - Charged Shot: Hold the fire button to charge up for a more powerful shot.

## Fireball Launcher

- Ammunition Type: Fireballs
- Firing Mode: Rapid fire, medium-range
- Range: Short to medium
- Description: The Fireball Launcher is a powerful weapon that shoots balls of fire at your enemies. These fireballs deal massive damage and can be used to clear out groups of enemies. Be cautious with its limited ammo and recharge time.
  - Special Features:
    - Splash Damage: Explodes on impact, dealing damage to enemies within the blast radius.
    - Fire Trail: The fireball leaves a fiery trail, potentially damaging enemies even if they don't directly get hit.

Doom Gun (Laser Rifle)

- Ammunition Type: Energy Cells
- Firing Mode: Single shots or continuous laser fire
- Range: Very long-range, with high accuracy
- Description: The Doom Gun is a high-tech laser rifle that can unleash devastating, continuous beams of energy. Its precision and long-range capabilities make it perfect for dealing with enemies from afar, especially in open areas where mobility is key.
    - Special Features:
        - Beam Mode: Hold the trigger to fire a continuous beam.
        - Charged Blast: Charge the shot to fire a devastating, concentrated laser blast.

Bomb Launcher

- Ammunition Type: Bombs (limited supply)
- Firing Mode: Launches explosive bombs in arcs
- Range: Medium to long, with arc trajectory
- Description: The Bomb Launcher launches explosive projectiles that deal massive area damage. These are especially useful for groups of enemies or large, powerful foes. While it has a slow reload speed, it can turn the tide of battle when used properly.
    - Special Features:
        - Timed Explosions: The bombs explode after a short delay or on impact.
        - Bouncing Bombs: Some bombs can bounce, making them effective for hitting enemies hiding behind cover.

*3.1.2 Melee Weapons*

Melee weapons are your go-to tools for close-quarters combat. Whether you're out of ammo or need to conserve resources, melee weapons let you slice, smash, and bash through enemies at close range. Here's a list of melee weapons you'll find in DOOM: The Dark Ages:

Sword of Flame

- Ammunition Type: None (melee)
- Firing Mode: Swing or charged attack
- Range: Short-range (close-quarters combat)
- Description: The Sword of Flame is a fiery blade that glows with magic. It's an incredibly powerful melee weapon, capable of cutting through enemies with ease. Its charged attack releases a fiery shockwave, hitting multiple enemies in its path.
  o Special Features:
    - Flame Burst: A charged attack that sends a burst of fire forward, damaging all enemies in the line of sight.
    - Bonus Damage: Deals increased damage to undead or demon-type enemies.

Axe of Destruction

- Ammunition Type: None (melee)
- Firing Mode: Swing with heavy impact
- Range: Short-range
- Description: The Axe of Destruction is a heavy weapon that's perfect for delivering devastating, powerful strikes. While slower than the sword, it deals much more damage with each swing, making it ideal for larger enemies or bosses.
  o Special Features:
    - Wide Swing: The axe's arc hits multiple enemies in its path.
    - Stun Effect: A fully charged swing can stun enemies, leaving them vulnerable for a few moments.

Whip of Shadows

- Ammunition Type: None (melee)
- Firing Mode: Lash or combo strikes
- Range: Medium-range (whip reach)
- Description: The Whip of Shadows is a versatile, quick weapon that strikes enemies at medium range. The whip can be used for both rapid combo attacks and reaching enemies at a distance. It's especially effective against agile foes and can even disarm or disorient them.
  - Special Features:
    - Chain Attack: The whip can lash enemies in quick succession, dealing damage over time.
    - Disarm: Use the whip to knock weapons out of enemies' hands or pull them closer.

Hammer of the Gods

- Ammunition Type: None (melee)
- Firing Mode: Heavy impact smash
- Range: Short-range, with shockwave effect
- Description: The Hammer of the Gods is a massive warhammer that can crush anything in its path. When swung, the hammer creates a shockwave that knocks enemies back and stuns them. It's perfect for clearing crowds of enemies in close-range combat.
  - Special Features:
    - Shockwave: Creates a blast radius that damages enemies near the point of impact.
    - Stagger Effect: Enemies hit by the hammer are briefly knocked down or stunned.

Fist of Power

- Ammunition Type: None (melee)
- Firing Mode: Punch, combo strikes, or charged hit
- Range: Close-range (melee)

- Description: The Fist of Power is an enchanted gauntlet that grants its wearer immense strength. With a single punch, you can send enemies flying, and with its charged attack, you can unleash an earth-shattering blow that impacts all nearby foes.
  - Special Features:
    - Shockwave Punch: A charged punch that sends a wave of force forward.
    - Knockback: Standard punches send enemies flying, useful for crowd control.

## 3.2 Combat Tips & Tricks

Mastering combat in DOOM: The Dark Ages requires a combination of strategic thinking, quick reflexes, and a deep understanding of the game's mechanics. From close-quarters brawls to large-scale firefights, this chapter will provide you with essential tips and tricks to help you become an unstoppable force against the legions of darkness.

### 3.2.1 Learn to Strafe and Dodge

One of the most essential skills in DOOM: The Dark Ages is strafe dodging. Enemies, especially the fast-moving or ranged ones, will try to overwhelm you with their attacks. To survive, you must constantly move and avoid their fire.

- Strafing: While shooting, use A and D (PC) or the Left Stick (console) to strafe. Moving sideways while aiming allows you to maintain fire while dodging incoming attacks.
- Dodge: For an added level of mobility, learn to use the dodge mechanic. On PC, you can bind the dodge button to a specific key (such as Shift), while on console it may be mapped to L1/LB or R1/RB. Use this to dodge enemy projectiles and get behind cover quickly.

Tip: Constant movement is key. Don't stay still, as standing still makes you an easy target. Always be moving while firing to minimize the chance of getting hit.

### 3.2.2 Use Cover Wisely

Many of the game's combat arenas include cover—such as pillars, walls, and obstacles—that can be used to your advantage. Use these structures to protect yourself from enemy fire and plan your next move.

- Peek and Shoot: Hide behind cover and pop out just enough to shoot, ensuring that you aren't fully exposed.
- Use Environments to Hide: If you're low on health or ammo, retreating to nearby cover can help you regroup. Don't forget to watch for health packs and ammo near cover to replenish your supplies.

Tip: Always check the environment for hidden spots to use as cover. Sometimes, there may be destructible walls or hidden paths that can give you an advantage.

### 3.2.3 Switch Weapons Quickly

In DOOM: The Dark Ages, you'll need to be able to switch between your weapons fast depending on the situation. For instance, a melee weapon might be useful in tight spaces, but you'll need your ranged weapon to deal with enemies at a distance.

- Weapon Wheel (PC): On PC, use the number keys or mouse scroll wheel to quickly switch between weapons. Alternatively, you can press Q (or another designated key) to bring up the weapon wheel and select the weapon of your choice.
- Weapon D-pad (Console): On consoles, use the D-pad to cycle between your weapons on the fly. Make sure you know the

order of your weapons so you can quickly grab the right one during combat.

Tip: Quick Weapon Switching is a game-changer. Practice switching between your primary and secondary weapons to maximize your combat efficiency. You can quickly fire a powerful weapon and then follow up with a melee strike or a different ranged attack for combos.

### 3.2.4 Learn Enemy Weaknesses

Different enemies in DOOM: The Dark Ages have different weaknesses. Some may be vulnerable to specific types of damage, while others may have special abilities or resistances. Knowing how to exploit these weaknesses will give you a huge advantage.

- Fire Vulnerability: Demons are typically weak to fire-based weapons. Use fireballs or flame-based attacks to melt through their defenses.
- Armor-Breaking Weapons: Some enemies have heavy armor or shields. To deal with these foes, use weapons that can penetrate armor, such as the Crossbow or Doom Gun with laser beams.
- Area-of-effect Weapons: For large groups of smaller enemies, use weapons that deal area-of-effect (AoE) damage, like the Bomb Launcher or Fireball Launcher.

Tip: Observe enemy behavior during combat. Take note of their attack patterns and the damage they take from different types of weapons. This will help you choose the right weapon for each encounter.

### 3.2.5 Use Power-ups and Items Strategically

Power-ups and consumables are vital to surviving the onslaught of enemies in DOOM: The Dark Ages. However, these items can be limited in number and may only appear at certain points in the game. Use them wisely.

- Health Packs: Don't waste health packs when you're at full health. Save them for moments when you're critically injured and need to survive a tough encounter.
- Armor: Armor absorbs damage, so make sure you pick up armor items whenever you can, especially before taking on tough enemies or bosses.
- Temporary Power-ups: Power-ups like invincibility or damage boosts should be saved for intense moments. Don't waste these boosts on weak enemies. Instead, wait until you're facing a boss or a large group of powerful enemies to maximize their effectiveness.

Tip: Before entering a big battle, scout the area for power-ups and item pickups. Ensure you're at full health, armor, and ammo before initiating any major combat sequences.

### 3.2.6 Time Your Melee Attacks

While ranged weapons offer precision and versatility, melee weapons are essential for dealing with enemies up close. DOOM: The Dark Ages features several melee weapons, each with unique effects and utility. However, timing your melee strikes is critical.

- Combo Attacks: Many melee weapons allow you to chain attacks together in quick succession. The Axe of Destruction and Fist of Power can deal devastating combos if you time your attacks correctly.
- Charged Attacks: Some melee weapons, like the Sword of Flame, have a charged attack that releases an area-of-effect (AoE) damage burst. Use these for crowd control when surrounded by multiple enemies.

Tip: Mix melee and ranged combat. When enemies close in on you, use melee weapons to knock them down, then switch back to your ranged weapons for more precise damage. This combination of weapon types allows you to manage a variety of combat situations.

### 3.2.7 Keep Moving During Boss Fights

Boss fights are some of the most intense and rewarding battles in DOOM: The Dark Ages. However, these encounters can be very difficult, especially when dealing with powerful bosses that have multiple phases and devastating attacks. Staying mobile is key to surviving these fights.

- Boss Mechanics: Each boss in DOOM: The Dark Ages will have unique attack patterns and weaknesses. Pay attention to their movements and projectiles so you can dodge their attacks effectively.
- Stay on the Move: Never stop moving during a boss fight. Use strafe dodging and rolls to avoid powerful attacks. Find and use cover whenever possible.
- Use the Arena: Many boss arenas are designed with special features, such as elevated platforms, destructible walls, or hidden paths. Use these to your advantage to avoid the boss's attacks and gain tactical positioning.

Tip: Learn the boss's attack patterns and make note of the best times to attack. When the boss is recovering or in between phases, that's your window to strike with everything you've got!

### 3.2.8 Experiment with Weapon Combinations

While each weapon in DOOM: The Dark Ages has its own strengths, combining certain weapons can yield even better results. For example, using explosive weapons like the Bomb Launcher followed by a melee attack with the Axe of Destruction can clear out large groups of enemies effectively.

- Ranged + Melee: When you've exhausted ammo, switch to your melee weapon to finish off stragglers or deal with close-range enemies.
- Elemental Combos: Certain weapons, like the Bow & Arrow, have elemental effects that can work in tandem with other weapons. For instance, using an elemental arrow and following it up with a fireball can incinerate enemies faster than using a single weapon.

Tip: Adapt your strategy depending on the situation. If you face a large group, you might want to use AoE weapons first, then switch to precise ranged weapons to clean up.

# 3.3 Managing Health and Armor

In DOOM: The Dark Ages, survival hinges on effectively managing both health and armor. These are your two primary resources for staying alive, and knowing when and how to use them can be the difference between life and death. This section will break down the essential strategies for keeping your health high and your armor intact while navigating through the dangerous world of DOOM: The Dark Ages.

*3.3.1 Health Management*

Your health is the most important resource in the game, and once it's depleted, your journey ends. Managing it effectively requires you to know when to fight and when to retreat, as well as how to find and use health items strategically.

- Health Pack Types:

- Small Health Pack: Restores a small amount of health.
- Large Health Pack: Restores a significant amount of health.
- Health Boosts: Temporary boosts that increase your maximum health for a limited time.

Tip: Use health items sparingly. When your health is low, make sure you're close to cover or safe zones before consuming health packs. It's better to save larger health packs for major battles or bosses.

### 3.3.2 Armor Management

Armor provides a layer of protection against enemy attacks and is crucial for surviving prolonged battles. Armor absorbs damage before it impacts your health, allowing you to take more hits. Just like health, armor is a finite resource, so it's important to use it wisely.

- Armor Types:
    - Basic Armor: Offers low protection but can be replenished easily throughout the game.
    - Heavy Armor: Provides higher damage resistance and is more difficult to find but can make a big difference during tough encounters.
    - Magical Armor: Offers special protective properties, such as resistance to elemental damage (fire, ice, etc.).

Tip: Keep an eye on your armor levels, especially before engaging in tough fights or large enemy hordes. When you're near full health but lack armor, use the armor-picking items to get back to full defensive capacity.

### 3.3.3 Health and Armor Item Location

Both health packs and armor items are often scattered throughout the environment. To maximize your chances of survival, learn to explore and remember key locations where these items are found.

- Exploration: Search rooms and areas for hidden health and armor supplies. Look for secret passages, destructible walls, or interactive objects that could lead to more supplies.
- Item Replenishment: Every time you clear an area or defeat a boss, check for health and armor replenishments. These items may spawn in safe rooms after a tough fight or boss encounter.

Tip: Always keep track of the health and armor regeneration points in each level. By knowing where to return for items, you can plan your exploration better and avoid getting caught in dire situations.

*3.3.4 Replenishing Health and Armor During Combat*

Sometimes you'll find yourself in the middle of combat with low health or no armor. Knowing how to manage and replenish these resources during battle is crucial.

- Speed and Efficiency: If you're low on health but have armor, focus on dodging attacks and staying out of range of powerful enemies while searching for health packs or safe spots to heal.
- Health Regeneration: In some levels, certain enemies or events might trigger health regeneration. Use these moments to restore your health, but beware of potential traps or ambushes.

Tip: Prioritize dodging and avoiding direct confrontation when health is low. If you're able to clear out minor enemies, you'll often find health and armor in the aftermath.

# 3.4 Enemy Types and Tactics

Understanding the enemy types in DOOM: The Dark Ages and their unique behaviors is key to surviving and defeating them. Each enemy requires a different approach and strategy. Whether you're facing basic minions or powerful bosses, knowing their strengths and weaknesses will give you the upper hand.

### 3.4.1 Basic Enemies

These are the common foes you'll encounter early in the game. While they may not pose an immediate threat on their own, their sheer numbers can overwhelm you.

- Zombie Warriors:
  - Behavior: Slow, melee-focused enemies.
  - Weakness: Vulnerable to all types of weapons, especially fire and magic.
  - Tactics: Keep your distance and pick them off with ranged weapons. If swarmed, use area-of-effect (AoE) attacks to clear them out quickly.
- Skeleton Archers:
  - Behavior: These enemies attack from a distance, firing arrows that deal moderate damage.
  - Weakness: Weak to melee attacks or fast projectiles.
  - Tactics: Close the gap quickly with melee weapons like the Sword of Flame or Whip of Shadows. If they're in groups, use area-of-effect attacks to clear them out.
- Imp Spawns:
  - Behavior: Fast, ranged enemies that throw fireballs at the player.
  - Weakness: Vulnerable to ice or water-based attacks.
  - Tactics: Avoid their projectiles by strafing. Use a Doom Gun or Crossbow to pick them off from a distance, or switch to fireproof armor if you need to close the gap for melee combat.

*3.4.2 Elite Enemies*

These are more powerful enemies that you will encounter later in the game. They have more health, stronger attacks, and usually require more strategy to defeat.

- Demon Knights:
    - Behavior: Heavily armored, slow-moving, and capable of both melee and ranged attacks. They are extremely durable and often have shields.
    - Weakness: Vulnerable to armor-piercing weapons like the Crossbow or Doom Gun.
    - Tactics: Focus on breaking their armor with your strongest ranged weapons. When they close the gap, use quick melee strikes to finish them off.
- Hellhounds:
    - Behavior: These demonic creatures are fast and aggressive, often hunting in packs.
    - Weakness: Weak to cold or lightning-based attacks.
    - Tactics: Keep moving constantly. Use ice arrows or the Bow & Arrow to slow them down. If they close in, switch to heavy melee weapons like the Axe of Destruction.
- Lich Sorcerer:
    - Behavior: Powerful magic users who can teleport and summon minions. They attack with devastating spells.
    - Weakness: Vulnerable to magical melee weapons like the Sword of Flame and fire-based attacks.
    - Tactics: Stay mobile to avoid their spells. Focus on interrupting their casting with melee combat or long-range magical projectiles.

### 3.4.3 Boss Enemies

Bosses are massive, powerful foes with unique attacks and phases. These enemies require strategy, preparation, and sometimes multiple attempts to defeat.

- The Demon Lord:
    - Behavior: A massive, multi-phase boss that teleports and summons minions. It uses fire and lava-based attacks.
    - Weakness: Weak to cold-based attacks and magic.
    - Tactics: Avoid the Demon Lord's lava blasts and summoned minions. Focus on dodging and use your fastest ranged weapons to attack from a distance. When it's vulnerable, unleash charged melee attacks.
- The Undying Tyrant:
    - Behavior: A necromantic boss that summons undead warriors and has a regeneration ability.
    - Weakness: Vulnerable to lightning and holy-based weapons.
    - Tactics: Use area-of-effect weapons to deal with summoned minions. For the boss itself, switch to lightning-based weapons to prevent regeneration. Don't let the Tyrant summon too many minions or you'll be overwhelmed.

### 3.4.4 General Enemy Tactics

- Keep Your Distance: Many enemies, especially ranged attackers, can be dealt with from afar. Use precision weapons like the Crossbow or Doom Gun.
- Environmental Awareness: Use the environment to your advantage. Many enemies have attack patterns that can be manipulated by cover or obstacles.

- Crowd Control: For large groups, use explosives or area-of-effect weapons to handle them efficiently. Bomb Launchers and Fireball Launchers can devastate groups.

# CHAPTER 4: EXPLORING THE DARK AGES WORLD

## 4.1 Level Design & Environment

The level design and environment in DOOM: The Dark Ages are key elements of the game's atmosphere and difficulty. Understanding how the environment interacts with gameplay can help you navigate challenging areas, find secret paths, and take advantage of environmental advantages to defeat enemies.

### 4.1.1 The Layout of Levels

Each level in DOOM: The Dark Ages is meticulously crafted with a mix of open spaces, tight corridors, verticality, and hidden areas. Some levels are straightforward, while others are complex, featuring multiple floors, secret passages, and nonlinear paths. Familiarizing yourself with these layouts will help you traverse levels with ease.

- Open Spaces: Large, wide-open areas are often where you'll face hordes of enemies or boss battles. These areas give you room to maneuver, but they may also be littered with hazards like lava pits, spikes, or falling platforms.
- Tight Corridors: Narrow spaces often force you to deal with close-range combat. Watch out for traps and ambushes when you enter these areas.
- Verticality: Some levels include multi-level structures or elevated platforms that require you to jump or climb to reach new areas. These can provide tactical advantages, such as high ground to shoot down on enemies or hidden loot.

Tip: Always pay attention to your mini-map or compass (if available). This can give you a general sense of where you need to go and whether you're near important locations like key rooms, boss battles, or secret paths.

*4.1.2 Interactive Environmental Elements*

The environments in DOOM: The Dark Ages are not just backdrops; they are integral to gameplay. Many levels contain interactive elements that you can manipulate to your advantage. From pressure plates to secret doors, the environment holds numerous opportunities for exploration.

- Lever Pulls & Pressure Plates: These often activate hidden doors or bridges. Be on the lookout for symbols or shapes on the ground to indicate where to step.
- Destructible Walls: Some walls or obstacles can be broken down to reveal hidden areas. Look for subtle differences in wall textures or cracked surfaces.
- Trap Triggers: Certain areas may have pressure-sensitive traps, like spikes, fire jets, or falling boulders. Use caution when stepping on suspicious spots or passing through narrow hallways.

Tip: Be sure to explore every room thoroughly, as hidden rooms often contain health, ammo, or armor that can be crucial in your survival.

*4.1.3 Dynamic Elements and Hazards*

Levels often feature dynamic elements and hazards that can alter the flow of gameplay. These include moving platforms, lava rivers, and rising water levels. Understanding how these work will help you avoid taking unnecessary damage and find the best way to progress through tricky areas.

- Lava and Acid Pools: Stepping into these will deal massive damage. Use platforms or jumping mechanics to cross these dangerous areas safely.
- Rising Water: Some levels feature flooded areas where the water level increases over time, making it harder to find dry ground. You may need to find air pockets or elevated platforms to survive.

Tip: When in hazardous areas, keep an eye on environmental cues (like rising water levels or flashing lights) to predict and avoid danger.


## 4.2 Key Locations and Areas

While the levels in DOOM: The Dark Ages are interconnected and expansive, there are several key locations and areas that stand out as critical to progression and offer significant rewards. Mastering these locations will ensure that you know where to go for specific objectives, whether it's a boss fight, treasure or unlockable paths.

### 4.2.1 Hub Areas

The hub serves as a central location where players can return to and access different parts of the game world. This area is usually safe from enemy attacks and provides the following:

- Fast Travel: You can access other areas or return to previously visited locations.
- Merchant or Vendor: Some hubs may feature a shopkeeper who offers weapons, upgrades, or health supplies in exchange for in-game currency or special items.
- Upgrade Stations: These stations allow you to upgrade weapons, abilities, or health/armor for enhanced performance.

Tip: Before leaving the hub, check the vendors and upgrade stations to ensure that you're fully prepared for the challenges ahead.

### 4.2.2 Key Locations for Progression

Throughout DOOM: The Dark Ages, there are a few key areas you'll need to visit to progress in the story and unlock new zones. These areas are often guarded by tough enemies or require solving puzzles to access.

- The Dark Castle: A towering stronghold that acts as a central point in the story. You'll need to defeat several powerful enemies before accessing the inner chambers.
- The Forgotten Caverns: A labyrinthine network of underground tunnels filled with monsters, traps, and puzzles. You'll need a special artifact to access the deeper parts.
- The Hellspire: A hellish tower where the final boss of the game resides. Before reaching the top, you must defeat the Four Horsemen of the apocalypse guarding each floor.

Tip: Pay attention to story clues and environmental hints to guide you toward these critical locations.

### 4.2.3 Secret Areas and Bonus Rooms

Secret areas are hidden throughout each level, often containing power-ups, hidden collectibles, and rare artifacts that help you on your journey. These areas can be unlocked by finding secret switches, performing specific actions, or simply exploring off the beaten path.

- Hidden Chambers: These rooms are often marked by obscure wall textures or hidden doors. They may contain bonus health, armor, or even extra weapons.
- Treasure Rooms: Hidden treasure chests or rooms that reward the player with unique artifacts or permanent upgrades to health or armor.

Tip: Keep an eye out for subtle environmental clues like cracks in the wall, unusual statues, or flickering torches that may indicate a hidden area.

## 4.3 Navigating Through Puzzles and Obstacles

The levels in DOOM: The Dark Ages aren't just about combat. Many areas require the player to solve puzzles or overcome obstacles in order to progress. Whether it's finding a hidden switch or figuring out how to bypass a giant door, your puzzle-solving skills will be put to the test.

### 4.3.1 Environmental Puzzles

Some levels are filled with puzzle elements that require observation and interaction with the environment to solve. These puzzles can involve anything from activating a series of pressure plates to finding hidden paths or triggering timed events.

- Pressure Plates and Switches: You may need to step on pressure plates or pull levers in the correct order to unlock doors or open hidden pathways.
- Color-coded Puzzles: In some areas, you'll find color-coded symbols or patterns that must be matched to open doors or release traps.

Tip: Examine the environment closely for clues. Often, puzzle elements are tied to the surrounding decor, such as mysterious inscriptions or glowing objects that give hints on what to do.

### 4.3.2 Timed Challenges and Obstacles

Many puzzles in DOOM: The Dark Ages are time-sensitive, requiring you to react quickly or face penalties, such as locked doors or enemy ambushes.

- Timed Platforms: These platforms will often sink or rise at specific intervals. You must time your jumps correctly to avoid falling into deadly traps or lava.
- Spinning Blades and Fire Jets: Moving obstacles, such as spinning blades or fire jets, create dangerous environments you must navigate carefully. Watch their patterns, and time your movements to avoid injury.

Tip: Before committing to a time-sensitive challenge, observe the movement patterns of the obstacles. Knowing when it's safe to move will prevent unnecessary damage.

### 4.3.3 Lever and Key Puzzles

In certain parts of the game, you'll need to use a specific item to interact with certain levers or unlock key mechanisms to progress. These may involve finding key items, such as mystical crystals, magical runes, or ancient books.

- Unlocking Doors: Some doors or pathways will require you to find the correct key or artifact. These items may be guarded by enemies or hidden in secret rooms.

Tip: Keep a mental note of important objects you find in each area, as you may need them later to solve puzzles or unlock doors.

# CHAPTER 5: ADVANCED STRATEGIES

## 5.1 Efficient Use of Ammo & Resources

In DOOM: The Dark Ages, resources like ammo, health, and armor are finite. Managing them effectively is crucial to survival, especially as you progress through more challenging levels. Understanding how to conserve and use these resources wisely will ensure you're always prepared for whatever the game throws at you.

### 5.1.1 Ammo Conservation

Ammo is one of the most precious resources in DOOM: The Dark Ages. Running out of bullets or magical charges at the wrong time can leave you vulnerable. Here's how to use your ammo efficiently:

- Know When to Use Your Weapons:
  - Ranged Weapons like crossbows and guns are powerful but can quickly deplete your ammo. Use them for tough enemies or boss fights where precision is needed.
  - For common enemies or minions, consider switching to melee attacks or less powerful weapons that don't use ammo, like the Whip of Shadows or Sword of Flame.
- Use Ammo Sparingly in Minor Fights:
  - Conserve your ammo by using melee weapons or environmental traps for standard enemies. Fire traps, explosive barrels, or falling rocks can quickly clear groups of enemies without wasting any ammo.
- Ammo Drops and Resupply:
  - Loot dropped by enemies or found in the environment is essential to maintaining your resources. Always keep

an eye out for ammo caches and weapon upgrades. Never leave a room without checking if any extra ammo has been dropped.

- Use Special Ammo Types Wisely:
    - Certain weapons, like the Doom Gun or Fireball Launcher, may use special ammo types. These should be used selectively and reserved for tougher enemies or bosses. You don't want to waste your explosive ammo on weaklings!

Tip: Keep a close watch on your ammo count. If you're running low, switch to a more efficient weapon (like a melee weapon or magic), and avoid using your most powerful firearms unless absolutely necessary.

### 5.1.2 Resource Management (Health & Armor)

In addition to ammo, managing health and armor is essential. These resources are just as important as your weapons for staying alive.

- Health Pack Efficiency:
    - Small health packs restore only a small amount of health, so save them for when you're just slightly hurt. Save large health packs for major injuries or critical situations.
- Armor:
    - Like health, armor helps you take hits without losing health. Always be on the lookout for armor upgrades or armor-picking items, especially before entering areas with tough enemies.
- When to Use Health & Armor:
    - Don't use a health pack unless you're in danger of dying, and avoid using armor when you're only missing a small amount. Try to combine them for maximum effectiveness, restoring both health and armor at the same time.
- Magical Resources:

- Certain weapons and powers require magical resources (mana, essence, etc.). Conserve these for high-stakes battles or when facing bosses. Don't waste them on weaker enemies when standard ammo will suffice.

Tip: Make sure to manage your resources regularly. For example, pick up health and armor immediately after combat to avoid leaving them behind. It's a good habit to constantly check your health, armor, and ammo at the beginning of each new area to prepare accordingly.

### 5.1.3 Environmental Resource Gathering

Throughout DOOM: The Dark Ages, certain environmental features or interactive objects provide natural resources. These can help reduce reliance on your limited supplies.

- Healing Pools: Some areas have healing pools or pools of water that gradually restore health over time. Keep track of these locations, especially if you're far from a health pack.
- Resupply Stations: Many levels have resupply stations or storage rooms where ammo, health, and armor are replenished. Be sure to locate these stations to restock before heading into dangerous areas.
- Environmental Hazards as Weapons:
  - Fire traps, explosive barrels, and other hazards can be used to your advantage. Use these traps to kill enemies without using any of your own resources.

Tip: Always explore the environment thoroughly. Even if you're low on resources, you can often find hidden healing items or ammo caches in tucked-away areas that can replenish your stock.

## 5.2 Boss Fights – Strategies and Tips

Boss battles are some of the most challenging and rewarding moments in DOOM: The Dark Ages. These enemies often have multiple phases, unique attack patterns, and require specific strategies to defeat. Here are some tips to help you conquer the biggest threats in the game.

### 5.2.1 Preparing for Boss Fights

Before heading into a boss fight, preparation is key. Here's what you should do to ensure success:

- Stock Up on Resources:
    - Make sure you have enough health and armor for the fight. You don't want to be running out of ammo or health during the battle.
    - Use health and armor packs strategically, and consider saving magical resources for special attacks.
- Choose the Right Weapon:
    - Some bosses are vulnerable to specific types of weapons. For instance, fire-based bosses may be weak to ice attacks, and undead bosses may be vulnerable to holy weapons.
    - If you're unsure, high-powered ranged weapons or melee weapons with strong knockback can deal significant damage.
- Save Special Ammo:
    - If you have access to powerful special ammo (like explosive rounds or magical projectiles), save them for boss phases when the boss is vulnerable or when you need to deal massive damage quickly.

Tip: Check the boss arena for any environmental elements you can use, such as explosive barrels or health fountains. These can help turn the tide of battle in your favor.

### 5.2.2 Identifying Boss Attack Patterns

Each boss in DOOM: The Dark Ages has unique attack patterns and abilities. Learning how to dodge or counter these attacks is vital to success.

- Dodge or Block Incoming Attacks:
    - Many bosses have charged-up attacks or area-of-effect (AoE) damage. Pay attention to their attack animations so you can dodge or block at the right time.
- Timing Special Attacks:
    - Bosses often have vulnerable phases after performing a special move or attack. During these moments, you can deal significant damage.
- Weak Points:
    - Certain bosses have weak points that require you to aim for specific areas, like their head, legs, or back. Identifying these weak points early can help you conserve ammo and focus on high-damage areas.

Tip: Study the boss's attack animation and timing. Bosses often have predictable patterns—once you recognize them, you'll be able to dodge, counterattack, and conserve resources more effectively.

### 5.2.3 Boss Phases and Changing Tactics

Many bosses in DOOM: The Dark Ages have multiple phases or stages to their battles, with each phase requiring a different approach. Here's how to adjust your strategy as the fight progresses:

- First Phase:

- o In the initial phase, bosses often use straightforward attacks and patterns. Focus on dodging and dealing consistent damage.
  - o Use basic ranged weapons to conserve special ammo for later phases.
- Second Phase:
  - o Bosses may change tactics in the second phase, introducing new attacks or minion summons. Be ready to dodge and stay mobile to avoid being overwhelmed.
  - o Use area-of-effect (AoE) attacks to deal with added minions or summons during this phase.
- Final Phase:
  - o The final phase is often the most difficult, with the boss using its most devastating abilities. This is the time to unleash your most powerful attacks and special ammo.
  - o Keep an eye on the environment for healing or armor items that may help you during this phase.

Tip: When entering the final phase, use your power-ups and special abilities. This is the moment to go all-out and finish off the boss.

*5.2.4 Common Boss Fights and Their Weaknesses*

- The Demon Lord: A massive demon with fire-based attacks. Weak to ice attacks and holy weapons.
  - o Strategy: Avoid fireballs and use ranged ice attacks or holy magic to chip away at its health. In the second phase, use explosive ammo to deal massive damage.
- The Undying Tyrant: An undead sorcerer who summons minions and regenerates health. Weak to lightning-based attacks.
  - o Strategy: Focus on minions in the first phase and save lightning-based weapons for the Tyrant in the second phase.
- The Lich Sorcerer: A magic-using boss with teleportation abilities. Weak to fire-based attacks.

o   Strategy: Dodge the sorcerer's projectile magic and hit him with fire-based weapons or area-of-effect magic when he teleports into a vulnerable position.

# 5.3 Advanced Weapon Upgrades & Customization

In DOOM: The Dark Ages, weapons are not only tools of destruction but also key components that can be enhanced and customized to suit your playstyle. Upgrading your arsenal is essential for staying competitive in the fight against increasingly powerful enemies. Here's how to maximize the effectiveness of your weapons and tailor them to your needs.

### 5.3.1 Weapon Upgrade Paths

Each weapon in DOOM: The Dark Ages has a series of upgrade paths that enhance its performance and add unique abilities. To unlock these upgrades, you'll need to find upgrade stations, crafting materials, or blueprints scattered throughout the game world.

- Basic Upgrades: These upgrades improve weapon damage, accuracy, or ammo capacity. They are the foundation for making your weapons more efficient.
- Elemental Enhancements: Some weapons can be modified with elemental effects like fire, ice, or lightning. These modifications make your weapons more effective against certain enemy types. For example, ice-based weapons are great for slowing down fast-moving enemies, while fire-based weapons excel against flesh-based monsters.
- Special Modifications: Some weapons have unique modifications that grant special abilities. For instance, the Doom Gun might have an upgrade path that turns it into a

charged energy weapon, while the Crossbow can be enhanced with explosive or poison-tipped bolts.

Tip: Focus on upgrading the weapons that you use most frequently. If you rely on long-range combat, prioritize accuracy and ammo capacity upgrades for guns. If you prefer close-quarters combat, invest in melee weapon upgrades or weapon durability.

### 5.3.2 Customizing Weapon Mods

In addition to upgrading weapons, weapon mods allow for more customization. These mods can alter the firing rate, fire modes, and other key characteristics of your weapons. You can swap mods at specific crafting stations or modular workbenches.

- Rapid Fire Mods: Increase the rate of fire for automatic weapons or energy weapons, making them more effective in crowd control situations.
- Zoom Mods: Improve your aiming accuracy and range with scopes or magnification sights. These are especially useful for sniping or dealing with distant enemies.
- Elemental Rounds: Modify your weapons to fire elemental projectiles that deal additional damage over time. For example, fire rounds ignite enemies, while frost rounds slow them down.
- Shotgun Mods: Some shotguns come with mods that can either fire spread shots for wide coverage or single projectiles for more precision. Experiment with these depending on the type of enemy and the environment.

Tip: Take advantage of environmental challenges when customizing your weapons. If you're entering an area with lots of fire hazards, an ice mod on your weapons might help you slow down enemies while keeping yourself at a safe distance.

*5.3.3 Crafting and Special Weapon Items*

Crafting is an essential aspect of weapon upgrades in DOOM: The Dark Ages. As you explore the world, you'll encounter crafting stations where you can combine rare materials, loot drops, and blueprints to create powerful weapons and ammo types.

- Legendary Weapons: Some legendary weapons require you to collect rare crafting materials from boss fights or hidden areas. These weapons are usually more powerful and come with unique abilities, such as summoning allies or teleportation effects.
- Custom Ammo Types: Certain crafting recipes allow you to create special ammo types, such as explosive shells, poisonous darts, or arcane magic projectiles. These can be used to target specific weaknesses of enemies or bosses.
- Ammo Compression: Upgrading your ammo capacity allows you to compress ammo into more compact forms, giving you more firepower with fewer shots.

Tip: Always be on the lookout for rare crafting materials. You can often find them in hidden rooms or after defeating powerful bosses. Stockpile these materials and craft legendary weapons when you have the resources.

## 5.4 Movement and Positioning Techniques

In DOOM: The Dark Ages, combat is not just about having powerful weapons—it's about being nimble, strategic, and always in control of your position. Movement and positioning are crucial to surviving and mastering the battlefield. Understanding how to use your surroundings and outmaneuver your enemies will ensure that you can defeat even the toughest foes.

*5.4.1 Mastering the Art of Movement*

The key to surviving in DOOM: The Dark Ages is fluid, fast-paced movement. While firing at enemies is important, positioning and dodging attacks are equally crucial for staying alive. Here's how to maximize your movement:

- Dodge and Roll: Utilize your dodge roll to quickly move in and out of combat. This is particularly useful when facing ranged enemies or bosses that have targeted attacks.
- Jumping and Double Jumping: Many levels feature platforms that require precision jumping. The ability to double jump allows you to reach high areas and avoid ground-based traps. This can give you a significant advantage in vertical combat situations.
- Mantling and Wall Running: Some areas of the game allow you to mantle over obstacles or wall run to reach otherwise inaccessible places. These skills are particularly useful when navigating complex environments or avoiding dangerous traps.
- Slide Dash: A slide dash technique allows you to dash forward in a crouched position, evading attacks and closing the distance between you and enemies. Use this technique to approach ranged enemies quickly or dodge melee attacks.

Tip: Keep moving! Standing still makes you an easy target. Mastering movement is essential, so get comfortable with dodging, jumping, and sliding to stay unpredictable and out of harm's way.

*5.4.2 Using the Environment to Your Advantage*

Positioning is not just about moving fast—it's about using the environment to control the flow of combat. Tactical positioning can be the difference between life and death in DOOM: The Dark Ages.

- High Ground Advantage: Always strive to take the high ground when possible. Being on elevated platforms gives you a better view of the battlefield and allows you to target enemies from a safer distance. Ranged weapons are especially effective when you have the high ground.

- Cover and Concealment: Use cover effectively during firefights. Pillars, walls, and other structures can shield you from incoming projectiles. Move between cover and keep an eye out for blind spots where enemies may ambush you.
- Environmental Traps: Many environments feature hazardous elements like lava pits, explosive barrels, and spikes. Position enemies near these traps to trigger environmental kills without wasting ammo.
- Choke Points: When fighting in narrow spaces, use choke points to your advantage. These are areas where you can funnel enemies and control the flow of combat. By bottlenecking enemies, you reduce the number of directions from which they can attack you.

Tip: Stay aware of your surroundings and look for ways to exploit environmental features. Use high ground, cover, and traps to gain the upper hand in any encounter.

### 5.4.3 Positioning Against Bosses and Tough Enemies

Positioning is particularly important when facing bosses or elite enemies in DOOM: The Dark Ages. These foes often have area-of-effect (AoE) attacks or can overwhelm you with sheer power, making strategic positioning essential for survival.

- Kiting: When fighting a boss, use kiting techniques to keep them at a distance. Move in and out of combat, ensuring that you're always in a position to dodge or counterattack.
- Aggro Management: Some bosses and enemies have aggressive attack patterns where they focus on one target at a time. Use this to your advantage by positioning yourself so that the boss is constantly facing away from you, allowing you to hit weak spots or deal damage.

- Boss Arena Utilization: Use the arena to your advantage. Some bosses have specific weaknesses tied to the environment. For example, a boss might be vulnerable to attacks while standing in a certain hazardous area, or there may be healing items in specific locations that you can use to your benefit.

Tip: Always be aware of your distance from the boss and adjust your positioning accordingly. When the boss begins a charge-up attack, move to the opposite side to avoid getting hit by its deadly blast.

# CHAPTER 6: ENEMIES & CREATURES OF THE DARK AGES

## 6.1 Overview of Foes You'll Face

In DOOM: The Dark Ages, you'll encounter a wide variety of enemies, ranging from mobs of low-tier minions to terrifying bosses. Each type of enemy has unique traits, weaknesses, and combat behaviors, which will challenge your strategy and test your combat skills. Understanding these enemies is the first step toward mastering the game.

### 6.1.1 Demonic Hordes

These enemies are the backbone of the DOOM: The Dark Ages universe. They come in a variety of shapes and sizes, but their common trait is their malevolent desire to destroy anything in their path.

- Imps: The most common enemies in the game. These small, fast creatures are armed with fireballs and possess quick reflexes. While they're weak individually, they can overwhelm you in large groups.
- Ghouls: Undead warriors that attack with razor-sharp claws. They're slower than Imps but can take more damage before going down.
- Hellhounds: Fast, vicious creatures that attack in packs. Their bite attacks deal substantial damage, and they can dodge projectiles with ease.

*6.1.2 Elemental Beasts*

These creatures are imbued with the powers of the natural elements. They have unique resistances and abilities, making them a challenge for players to deal with.

- Fire Elementals: These enemies appear as living flames. They're immune to fire damage but weak to ice and water-based attacks.
- Ice Titans: Large, imposing creatures made of ice and snow. They can freeze players in place with their frost breath and are highly resistant to physical damage, but vulnerable to fire.
- Storm Wraiths: Aerial creatures that wield lightning. They can zap you from a distance and teleport around the arena. They're most vulnerable to earth-based attacks.

*6.1.3 Undead Legions*

The undead are some of the most insidious and dangerous enemies in DOOM: The Dark Ages, for they rise from the graves and attack relentlessly.

- Skeleton Warriors: Clad in tattered armor, these sword-wielding foes can be tough to kill, but they are very slow. Focus on decapitating them for a quick kill.
- Liches: Powerful necromancers that can summon undead minions and cast dark spells. They're weak in direct combat, but their spellcasting abilities make them deadly from a distance.
- Vampires: Fast-moving, stealthy enemies that drain your health with each attack. Their regeneration abilities make them hard to deal with unless you have holy-based weapons.

*6.1.4 Mythical Giants*

These enemies are massive, ancient creatures that are often tied to the lore of the world. Their size and power make them formidable adversaries.

- Trolls: Large, heavily armored creatures that wield massive clubs or stone boulders. Their high health pool and heavy armor make them tough to defeat, but they're slow and vulnerable to magic.
- Giants of Stone: These hulking creatures have rock-hard skin and can cause earthquakes when they slam the ground. They're immune to most physical attacks, but can be damaged by elemental or explosive weapons.
- Dragonkin: Powerful dragon-like creatures with fire breath and razor-sharp claws. They're highly dangerous but can be brought down with ranged fire-based weapons or magic.

## 6.2 Best Ways to Counter Each Enemy

Each type of enemy in DOOM: The Dark Ages has its own weaknesses and combat strategies. Knowing how to effectively counter each enemy type is key to surviving the dark, treacherous world. Below are some tips on how to counter specific foes.

*6.2.1 Countering Demonic Hordes*

- Imps:
  - Strategy: Use fast-firing, accurate weapons like the Crossbow or Short Sword. Keep moving to avoid their fireball attacks, and take out groups with explosive weapons like grenades or fire-based magic.
  - Weakness: Weak to holy weapons and explosives.
- Ghouls:

- Strategy: Use fire-based weapons to burn them down quickly. Be sure to stay at a distance, as their claw attacks can deal heavy damage in close-quarters combat.
- Weakness: Vulnerable to fire, resistant to ice and water-based attacks.
- Hellhounds:
  - Strategy: Stay mobile and use ranged weapons to keep them at bay. If fighting in a confined area, use explosives or traps to deal with groups.
  - Weakness: Weak to poison and magic-based attacks.

### 6.2.2 Countering Elemental Beasts

- Fire Elementals:
  - Strategy: Ice weapons are your best bet here, as they can freeze the fire elementals and neutralize their attack range. Avoid staying too close to these creatures, as their fireball attacks can deal heavy damage.
  - Weakness: Ice-based weapons, water, and arcane magic.
- Ice Titans:
  - Strategy: Use fire-based weapons or explosive attacks to melt the ice. Keep your distance and avoid their frost breath by constantly moving and using dash maneuvers.
  - Weakness: Weak to fire-based weapons and explosives.
- Storm Wraiths:
  - Strategy: Use earth-based magic or melee weapons with electrical resistance to ground them. Watch out for their teleportation abilities, and don't let them get too close to you.
  - Weakness: Earth-based magic or melee combat with lightning resistance.

### 6.2.3 Countering Undead Legions

- Skeleton Warriors:
  - Strategy: Use magic attacks or holy weapons to deal extra damage to the undead. Their sword swings are easily dodged, so focus on quick strikes and decapitation.
  - Weakness: Vulnerable to holy-based weapons and explosives.
- Liches:
  - Strategy: Keep a distance and avoid their summoning spells. Use lightning or fire-based weapons to counter their dark magic. Make sure to interrupt their casting with ranged attacks.
  - Weakness: Weak to lightning-based or fire-based attacks.
- Vampires:
  - Strategy: Use holy weapons to stop their regeneration, or hit them with lightning-based weapons to paralyze them temporarily. Avoid being cornered, as their bite attacks drain your health.
  - Weakness: Vulnerable to holy-based attacks and lightning.

### 6.2.4 Countering Mythical Giants

- Trolls:
  - Strategy: Use elemental magic or ranged attacks to break through their armor. Melee combat is not recommended, as their large clubs can deal heavy damage, but they are slow and can be outmaneuvered.
  - Weakness: Weak to magic, especially fire and lightning.
- Giants of Stone:
  - Strategy: Keep your distance and use explosive attacks to deal high damage. Elemental magic can break through their stone armor, but it will take time to weaken them.

- o Weakness: Weak to explosives and elemental magic.
- Dragonkin:
  - o Strategy: Avoid their fire breath by staying close to cover or using shielding spells. Ranged weapons like bows or crossbows work best to bring them down from a distance.
  - o Weakness: Vulnerable to magic and ranged attacks.

# 6.3 Special Abilities of Creatures

Each enemy in DOOM: The Dark Ages is equipped with unique special abilities that make them a formidable challenge. Understanding these abilities will help you devise strategies to deal with them effectively.

*6.3.1 Fire Elementals' Inferno Surge*

- Ability: Fire Elementals can channel an Inferno Surge, a wide-reaching flame attack that engulfs the area in a massive fire blast.
- Counter: Use ice-based weapons or water magic to negate the effects. Keep your distance, and be ready to dodge quickly.

*6.3.2 Ice Titan's Frost Breath*

- Ability: The Ice Titan's Frost Breath can freeze players in place, making them vulnerable to follow-up attacks.
- Counter: Use fire-based attacks to melt the ice, or keep moving to avoid being hit by its chilling effects.

*6.3.3 Lich's Dark Summon*

- Ability: Liches have the power to summon undead minions to overwhelm players during battle.

- Counter: Focus on eliminating the Lich first, as it has lower health. Holy weapons can also disrupt the summoning process.

### 6.3.4 Dragonkin's Firestorm

- Ability: The Dragonkin unleashes a Firestorm, raining fire down on the battlefield and dealing massive area damage.
- Counter: Dodge the fireballs or use shield spells to absorb the damage. Avoid open areas and take cover to minimize damage.

# CHAPTER 7: WEAPONS AND POWER-UPS

## 7.1 Overview of Weapons

In DOOM: The Dark Ages, your weapons are your primary tools for survival. From standard firearms to magical artifacts, each weapon plays a vital role in your combat strategy. Understanding the different categories of weapons and their uses will ensure that you're always equipped for whatever threat lies ahead.

### 7.1.1 Standard Weapons

Standard weapons are your bread and butter in DOOM: The Dark Ages. They are versatile, reliable, and suited for a wide range of combat scenarios. These weapons are easy to find and form the core of your arsenal.

- Sword of Flame: A one-handed melee weapon imbued with fire magic. It's perfect for dealing with close-range enemies and can deal significant damage in rapid succession. The sword also has a special attack: a fire burst that hits all enemies in its immediate vicinity.
    - Best Used For: Close-range combat with enemies such as Ghouls, Imps, and Hellhounds.
    - Weakness: Weak against frost-based enemies (like Ice Titans).
- Crossbow: A ranged weapon with the ability to fire explosive or poison-tipped bolts. The crossbow has excellent accuracy and a powerful rate of fire, making it useful for taking out enemies at medium distances.
    - Best Used For: Long-range combat and traps for kiting enemies.

- o Weakness: Slower reload time compared to other ranged weapons.
- Flintlock Pistol: A classic firearm, the Flintlock Pistol delivers steady damage with a fast rate of fire. It's a great all-rounder for medium-range combat and offers quick reload speed.
    - o Best Used For: Medium-range combat and dealing with mobs.
    - o Weakness: Limited ammo capacity and lower damage against tougher enemies.
- Heavy Hammer: A large, two-handed weapon designed for melee combat. It deals high physical damage and has a special stun effect that temporarily incapacitates enemies.
    - o Best Used For: Tanking and crowd control in tight spaces.
    - o Weakness: Slow attack speed and vulnerable to ranged enemies.
- Basic Wand: A simple magic wand that can cast basic arcane spells such as projectile blasts and shielding spells. It's a reliable tool for early-game magic and is essential for those who wish to specialize in magic combat.
    - o Best Used For: Low-level magic attacks and supportive spells.
    - o Weakness: Low damage output and requires mana to function.

### 7.1.2 Rare and Special Weapons

Rare and special weapons are harder to come by but offer unique advantages that make them invaluable for taking down stronger enemies and bosses. These weapons often come with magical properties or advanced technologies that give them distinct powers.

- Doom Gun: A devastating weapon with the ability to channel raw chaos energy into explosive projectiles. The Doom Gun has both a high damage output and a special energy blast that can destroy multiple enemies in one shot. However, it requires special ammunition that is hard to come by.

- o Best Used For: Boss fights and high-damage output in tight situations.
  - o Weakness: Limited ammo supply and slow reload.
- Elemental Staff: A mystical staff that can channel the power of the four elements: fire, ice, lightning, and earth. Each element offers a unique ability: fireball for damage, frost breath for slowing enemies, lightning for chain damage, and earthquake for area damage. The staff is perfect for those who prefer a diverse magic arsenal.
  - o Best Used For: Versatile magic attacks and crowd control.
  - o Weakness: Mana cost is high for certain elemental spells.
- Vampire's Fang: A rare melee weapon that grants the wielder the ability to drain health from enemies with every strike. This sword not only delivers damage but also replenishes the user's health, making it ideal for prolonged battles.
  - o Best Used For: Sustained combat and health regeneration during fights.
  - o Weakness: Low damage output compared to other heavy weapons.
- Shadow Bow: A unique bow that fires shadow arrows. These arrows can pass through solid objects and disintegrate enemies on impact, making them perfect for taking out enemies hiding behind cover. The bow also has a special ability to teleport the player to the location of any arrow after firing.
  - o Best Used For: Precision shots and long-range attacks against hidden enemies.
  - o Weakness: Low rate of fire and requires rare arrows.
- Holy Blade: A two-handed sword imbued with holy energy, capable of smiting undead creatures and demons. It has a special aura that damages enemies in close proximity and offers temporary invincibility when wielded.
  - o Best Used For: Boss fights against undead enemies and demonic foes.
  - o Weakness: Heavy and slow attack speed compared to lighter melee weapons.

- Arcane Gun: A magical firearm that fires magic-infused bullets capable of bypassing armor. It also has the ability to slow down time temporarily when fully charged, allowing you to dodge enemy attacks and target weak spots with precision.
    - Best Used For: Precision targeting and time manipulation during combat.
    - Weakness: Low ammo capacity and requires time to charge.
- Dragon's Claw: A unique ranged weapon that fires dragonfire projectiles. These projectiles cause explosive bursts and leave lingering fire damage over time. It's the ultimate weapon for those who want to deal massive AoE damage.
    - Best Used For: Area-of-effect damage and high DPS against groups of enemies.
    - Weakness: Slow reload and high ammo consumption.

## 7.2 Power-ups and How to Maximize Their Potential

Power-ups are temporary boosts that can give you a significant advantage in DOOM: The Dark Ages. From increased damage output to enhanced defenses, these items can be the difference between life and death in tough battles. Understanding when and how to use them will help you maximize their potential and increase your survival rate.

*7.2.1 Types of Power-ups*

- Berserker Rage: This power-up greatly increases your melee damage and allows you to stun enemies with each hit. It's perfect for taking down swarms of enemies or fighting tough bosses up close.
    - Maximize Potential: Use this when you're surrounded by low-tier enemies or need to break through enemy

lines quickly. Focus on chain attacking to maximize the damage dealt.

- Invisibility Cloak: Grants temporary invisibility, allowing you to move undetected by enemies. This is useful for stealth kills, avoiding direct combat, or setting up ambushes.
    o Maximize Potential: Use it to sneak past hordes or line up headshots with ranged weapons. Keep an eye on the duration of the effect, as the cloak is short-lived. Don't get too close to enemies or risk breaking your invisibility.
- Speed Boost: This power-up increases your movement speed and dodge effectiveness. You'll be able to avoid attacks more easily and move around the battlefield with greater agility.
    o Maximize Potential: Combine with long-range weapons or magic spells for better maneuverability. When fighting bosses, this can help you avoid their most devastating attacks while still dealing damage.
- Damage Boost: Temporarily increases your overall damage output across all weapons. This power-up is invaluable in situations where you need to deal high damage quickly, such as when facing boss enemies or high-health enemies like giants.
    o Maximize Potential: Activate it right before engaging bosses or high-damage foes. Pair it with high-damage weapons like the Doom Gun or Holy Blade for maximum damage.
- Health Regeneration: Slowly regenerates a portion of your health over time. It's a great way to recover between fights or in between areas where healing resources are scarce.
    o Maximize Potential: Use this when you're exploring or navigating low-risk areas, but avoid relying on it in the heat of combat, as its effect is gradual. Combine with mana potions if you're using a lot of magic to stay at full health.
- Armor Enhancement: Temporarily boosts your armor resistance, making you more resistant to damage from both physical and elemental sources. This power-up is ideal for surviving against high-damage enemies and bosses.

- Maximize Potential: Activate when you're about to enter combat with tough enemies or bosses. This will allow you to absorb more damage and stay in the fight longer. It's especially effective when paired with defensive weapons like the Shield Wand.
- Mana Infusion: Instantly refills your mana, allowing you to cast more spells. This is a crucial power-up for mages or anyone using magic-based combat.
  - Maximize Potential: Use this power-up when your mana is low and you need to unleash a powerful spell or escape with defensive magic. Spell-heavy classes can benefit the most, but it can also help casters maintain sustained damage during boss fights.

## 7.2.2 Power-up Strategies

- Timing is Key: Power-ups are only useful when you activate them at the right moment. Save power-ups like Damage Boost and Berserker Rage for tough encounters, such as boss battles or high-density enemy hordes.
- Use In Combination: Many power-ups can be used together for maximum impact. For example, using Speed Boost and Damage Boost simultaneously can make you an unstoppable force of destruction.
- Conserve for Boss Fights: While it's tempting to use power-ups as soon as you find them, try to save them for boss fights or other high-stakes situations. This ensures that you get the most out of the power-up's effect when it really counts.
- Avoid Waste: Make sure you use power-ups efficiently. If you're at full health or armor, holding off on health regeneration and armor boosts might be a good idea until your resources deplete.

## 7.3    Weapon Upgrades and Modifications

Weapon upgrades and modifications are a crucial part of progressing in DOOM: The Dark Ages. As you advance, you'll unlock the ability to improve your weapons, making them more powerful, versatile, and tailored to your playstyle. Upgrades can come in the form of new abilities, enhanced damage, or even additional effects that give you the edge in battle.

### 7.3.1 Types of Weapon Upgrades

- Increased Damage: One of the most straightforward upgrades, increasing the damage output of your weapons. This is essential for taking down tougher enemies and bosses more quickly.
    - Maximize Potential: Upgrade high-tier weapons like the Doom Gun or Holy Blade to increase your overall kill speed against powerful foes.
- Faster Reload: Reduces the time it takes to reload certain ranged weapons, improving the flow of combat and allowing you to fire more rounds in less time.
    - Maximize Potential: Focus on upgrading crossbows or firearms for a quicker and more efficient rate of fire.
- Elemental Modifications: Certain weapons can be enhanced with elemental properties such as fire, ice, electricity, or poison. These modifications allow you to deal additional elemental damage to enemies.
    - Maximize Potential: Use elemental modifications on weapons like the Crossbow or Arcane Gun to exploit enemy weaknesses. For example, fire-based weapons are highly effective against undead or frost-based enemies.
- Extended Magazines: Increasing the ammo capacity of your ranged weapons allows you to keep fighting longer without the need to reload. This is particularly useful for high-rate-of-fire weapons.

- o Maximize Potential: Use this upgrade on weapons like the Flintlock Pistol or Arcane Gun to keep enemies at bay while minimizing downtime between shots.
- Precision Sights: Adding optical sights or scopes to your weapons increases their accuracy, allowing you to target weak spots on enemies more effectively.
  - o Maximize Potential: Long-range weapons such as the Crossbow or Shadow Bow will benefit most from these modifications, allowing you to take out enemies from afar with greater precision.
- Explosive Rounds: Some ranged weapons can be upgraded to shoot explosive rounds, which deal area-of-effect damage. This is perfect for dealing with large groups of enemies or bosses that summon minions.
  - o Maximize Potential: Use these modifications for weapons like the Flintlock Pistol or Crossbow to maximize your crowd control capabilities.
- Elemental Shields: Magical shields can be applied to certain weapons, granting the wielder temporary resistance to elemental damage or reflecting incoming projectiles.
  - o Maximize Potential: Apply these to melee weapons like the Heavy Hammer or Holy Blade to increase your survivability during tough battles with elemental creatures.

### 7.3.2 How to Acquire Weapon Upgrades

- Find Upgrade Stations: Throughout the game, you will come across upgrade stations where you can apply modifications to your weapons. These stations are often hidden in secret rooms or areas that require special keys or actions to unlock.
- Crafting Materials: Some upgrades require crafting materials that you'll collect as you explore. These materials can be obtained by defeating bosses, completing side quests, or scavenging in dungeons.

- Progression Rewards: As you level up or complete key quests, you'll be rewarded with upgrade points or modular parts that can be used to unlock advanced upgrades for your weapons.

### 7.3.3 Upgrade Strategies

- Specialize Your Playstyle: Focus on upgrading weapons that match your combat style. If you prefer melee combat, upgrade your sword or heavy weapons. If you like ranged combat, focus on upgrading crossbows, pistols, or magic wands.
- Balance Upgrades: Don't just upgrade one weapon; balance your upgrades across multiple weapon types so you're prepared for any combat situation. For instance, upgrading both a ranged weapon and a melee weapon allows you to handle close and long-range threats.
- Prioritize Damage and Ammo: If you're frequently running out of ammo, consider upgrading the capacity of your weapons. If you're struggling to deal enough damage, prioritize damage upgrades and explosive rounds to maximize your output.

# CHAPER 8: MULTIPLAYER (IF APPLICABLE)

## 8.1 Setting Up Multiplayer

In DOOM: The Dark Ages, multiplayer offers an exhilarating experience where you can face off against other players or team up for cooperative missions. Setting up multiplayer properly ensures smooth gameplay, whether you're diving into intense PvP battles or coordinating with others in co-op campaigns.

*8.1.1 Multiplayer Setup Options*

- Online Multiplayer: To play online, ensure you have a stable internet connection. You can either create a lobby for your friends or join an open server. DOOM: The Dark Ages supports cross-platform play, allowing players from different platforms (PC, console, etc.) to compete or cooperate together.
- Local Multiplayer: If you prefer to play with friends at home, split-screen multiplayer is available. You can connect multiple controllers to your device and play together on a single screen. This mode is perfect for couch co-op or competitive play with friends.
- Co-op Mode Setup: If you're more into cooperative gameplay, you can select Co-op Campaign from the multiplayer menu. This mode allows you to play through the game's missions with friends, tackling enemies and bosses as a team. To ensure a good experience, make sure all players are running the same version of the game and have compatible game settings.
- Private vs Public Sessions: You can set up your multiplayer session to be private or public:
    - Private: Invite-only sessions where you control who joins the game.

      o   Public: Open lobbies where anyone can join, ideal for spontaneous multiplayer sessions.

*8.1.2 Joining Multiplayer Sessions*

- Inviting Friends: To invite friends to your session, open your friends list in the game menu and select their names. Once they accept your invitation, they'll be able to join your game directly.
- Joining Open Lobbies: If you're looking for random opponents or teammates, you can browse public lobbies where others are waiting to play. You can filter lobbies by game type, map, and region to find the best matches.

## 8.2 Game Modes and How to Play

In DOOM: The Dark Ages, multiplayer is packed with various game modes that cater to different playstyles. Whether you're looking for fast-paced PvP or strategic co-op missions, there's something for everyone.

*8.2.1 Multiplayer Game Modes*

- Deathmatch: The classic PvP mode where players fight to the death in a free-for-all arena. Each player starts with basic weapons and must gather additional ammo and power-ups to survive. The player with the most kills at the end of the match wins.
  - o   Strategy Tip: Focus on map control to grab power-ups first and make sure to avoid bottlenecks where enemies might be camping. Movement and positioning are key.

- Team Deathmatch: A team-based version of Deathmatch where players are divided into teams. The first team to score a set number of kills wins.
  - Strategy Tip: Coordinate with your teammates and focus on teamwork. Stay close to teammates for support and utilize combo attacks to take down enemies more efficiently.
- Capture the Flag (CTF): A mode where two teams battle to capture the opposing team's flag and return it to their base. The defending team must prevent the flag carrier from escaping, while the attacking team works to retrieve the flag and bring it back to their base.
  - Strategy Tip: Assign specific roles to teammates (e.g., defender, flag carrier, support). Use distraction tactics to confuse the enemy team and create openings for the flag carrier.
- King of the Hill: Players or teams compete for control of a central area (the Hill). The team or player who holds the area for the longest amount of time wins.
  - Strategy Tip: Use crowd control weapons to keep opponents out of the hill area. Be aware of your positioning and try to stay in the center of the hill to ensure full points.
- Co-op Campaign: Play through the game's story missions with friends. Each player can take on a different role, allowing you to utilize different strategies and weapon loadouts as a team.
  - Strategy Tip: Coordinate your actions with your teammates and choose complementary classes (e.g., having one player focus on tank, another on damage, and the third on support/healing).
- Survival Mode: Fight against waves of enemies that become progressively harder. Survive as long as you can, with the goal being to achieve the longest survival time.
  - Strategy Tip: Maximize weapon and power-up usage by saving ammo and resources. Stay mobile and always watch your health and armor—use health stations wisely and communicate with your team.

- Boss Rush: A mode where players face off against multiple bosses in succession, each more challenging than the last. Success depends on team coordination, weapon choices, and power-up management.
  - Strategy Tip: Focus on high DPS weapons and keep an eye on boss mechanics. Use coordinated strategies to avoid getting overwhelmed and tackle bosses one at a time.

# 8.3 Multiplayer Strategy Guide

Multiplayer in DOOM: The Dark Ages is fast-paced and requires a combination of skill, strategy, and teamwork. Here are key strategies for success in various multiplayer modes:

*8.3.1 General Multiplayer Tips*

- Map Awareness: Knowing the layout of each map is crucial. Be familiar with high-traffic areas, power-up locations, and escape routes. In Team Deathmatch, positioning is key—use your environment to your advantage.
- Resource Management: Manage your ammo, health, and armor wisely. Don't waste powerful weapons unless you're sure it's necessary. Power-ups should be timed for critical moments.
- Speed and Mobility: Movement is as important as shooting. Master dodging, jumping, and using cover to avoid taking damage. Speed boosts and teleportation can help you escape tough situations.
- Sound Awareness: In multiplayer, listening for enemy movement can give you a huge advantage. Pay attention to footsteps, gunfire, and other sound cues to anticipate enemy movements.

- Use Voice Chat/Signals: Communication is vital in multiplayer, especially in team modes. Use voice chat to coordinate with teammates, call out enemy positions, and strategize in real-time. In co-op modes, assign roles and be prepared to adapt.

*8.3.2 Specific Mode Strategies*

- Deathmatch:
    - Keep moving: Stay unpredictable, and never stand still. Avoid choke points and always be aware of high ground positions.
    - Control power-ups: Master where power-ups spawn and grab them early to give you an advantage over your enemies.
    - Don't be afraid to retreat: If you're low on health or ammo, don't hesitate to back off and regroup. Wait for a good opportunity to attack again.
- Capture the Flag:
    - Assign clear roles: One or two players should focus on defending the flag, while others should work on offense to capture the enemy flag.
    - Speed is key: The flag carrier should have a quick escape route planned and use speed boosts to dodge enemy pursuers.
    - Use distractions: Create chaos in the enemy base to pull attention away from the flag carrier.
- King of the Hill:
    - Dominate the Hill: Stay in the central area as much as possible and use defensive strategies like area denial weapons to keep enemies from entering the Hill.
    - Coordinate with your team: Set up perimeter defenses and have ranged players support the hillholder.
- Co-op Campaign:
    - Team synergy: Assign players to roles—someone to tank damage, another to deal damage, and someone to focus on support or healing.

- Reviving teammates: Always help fallen teammates as quickly as possible. Group up when things get tough and don't be afraid to fall back if necessary.
- Survival Mode:
  - Conserve ammo: In later waves, you'll face more enemies, so don't waste ammo on weaklings. Use melee weapons when possible.
  - Keep moving: Never let yourself get cornered, and always have an exit strategy. Prioritize area control and strongholds.

# CHAPTER 9: SECRETS, EASTER EGGS, AND HIDDEN FEATURES

## 9.1 Unlockable Secrets in Each Level

In DOOM: The Dark Ages, the levels are packed with hidden secrets that can reward players with powerful items, hidden paths, and bonus objectives. These secrets can make a significant difference in your progress, offering you much-needed advantages in combat, health, and ammunition. Here's how you can uncover some of the most elusive secrets in the game:

*9.1.1 Types of Unlockable Secrets*

- Hidden Rooms: Many levels contain secret rooms that are either hidden behind false walls or require a specific action to reveal. These rooms often contain health packs, armor, and powerful weapon upgrades.
  - Example: In the Cavern of Shadows, a hidden switch can open a concealed wall that leads to a treasure room filled with mana potions and weapon upgrades.
- Secret Objectives: Some levels offer bonus objectives that, when completed, unlock special content such as artifacts, unlockable weapons, or unique abilities. These objectives are often hidden, requiring players to solve puzzles or defeat certain enemies under specific conditions.
  - Example: In The Ruins of Norn, finding all ancient sigils scattered throughout the level unlocks the Hidden Tome of Knowledge, a powerful artifact that enhances your spellcasting abilities.

- Hidden Areas: Certain levels have out-of-sight areas that may not be immediately apparent. These could be hidden passages that lead to shortcuts, bonus levels, or special rewards.
    - Example: In the Crypt of Eternal Night, look for a series of cryptic inscriptions that hint at the location of a secret passage that opens up to a hidden boss fight.

*9.1.2 How to Find Secrets*

- Look for Clues: Hidden secrets are often telegraphed through environmental clues. These could be oddly placed crates, suspicious walls, or even unusual sounds that hint at something nearby. Pay close attention to these to spot secrets you might otherwise miss.
- Interact with the Environment: Many secrets are revealed by interacting with the environment. This could include pressing hidden switches, shooting specific objects, or standing on hidden platforms that trigger doors or walls to open.
- Explore Thoroughly: Secrets aren't always obvious. Be sure to explore every nook and cranny of each level. Backtrack if necessary, as sometimes a secret area can only be accessed after progressing through the level a little further.

## 9.2   Hidden Weapons and Power-ups

Throughout DOOM: The Dark Ages, there are several hidden weapons and power-ups scattered across the levels. These items can provide a major advantage in combat, and discovering them is key to surviving the increasingly difficult enemies.

### 9.2.1 Hidden Weapons

- Hellfire Bow: A powerful ranged weapon that fires fire-infused arrows, causing significant damage over time. It's hidden in the Ruins of Eldrad, behind a series of pressure plates that need to be activated in the correct order.
    - Usage Tip: Ideal for taking down tough enemies or bosses due to its high DPS and area-of-effect flame damage.
- Doom Gun: A legendary weapon that can obliterate enemies with a single shot. It's hidden in the Temple of the Unseen, and players must complete a series of puzzle challenges and defeat a secret boss to acquire it.
    - Usage Tip: Best used against bosses and high-health enemies. Its slow reload is a trade-off for its massive damage output.
- Excalibur Sword: This mystical sword is imbued with the power of the ancient gods and is found in the Cavern of Sorrows. To unlock it, you need to perform a ritual by sacrificing enemies in a specific order.
    - Usage Tip: A powerful melee weapon with a large area-of-effect. Perfect for crowd control when surrounded by hordes of weaker enemies.

### 9.2.2 Hidden Power-ups

- Berserker Mask: Temporarily boosts melee damage and gives the player the ability to stun enemies with each attack. Hidden in the Doomsworn Fortress, this power-up is obtained by finding and completing a series of combat trials.
    - Usage Tip: Combine with speed boosts to clear large groups of enemies quickly. This is especially useful in boss fights where rapid, high-damage attacks can overwhelm powerful foes.
- Phoenix Feather: This power-up gives players the ability to resurrect once when killed. Hidden in the Frostbite Cavern, it

can only be accessed by solving an environmental puzzle that involves navigating through ice mazes.

- o Usage Tip: A game-changer in tougher levels. Use it strategically when you're about to face a challenging boss or a particularly dangerous enemy.
- Divine Shield: This power-up provides temporary invulnerability and is hidden within the Eternal Fortress. The shield can block incoming attacks from all sources, allowing you to focus on offense without worrying about defense.
  - o Usage Tip: Activate before rushing into large battles or during boss encounters to avoid taking damage while you unleash your most powerful attacks.

## 9.3 Easter Eggs and References to the Doom Universe

DOOM: The Dark Ages is filled with references to the classic DOOM universe, offering a fun experience for longtime fans of the series. These Easter eggs are hidden throughout the game and can provide a unique, nostalgic experience.

### 9.3.1 Classic DOOM References

- Classic DOOM Iconography: Throughout the game, you may find posters, graffiti, or symbols referencing the original DOOM games. For example, a skull-faced symbol in the Hellish Descent level pays homage to the DOOM Slayer's iconic logo.
- DOOM Marine Statue: In the Ancient Ruins, there's a hidden statue of the DOOM Marine, the iconic character from the DOOM series. Activating the statue will reveal a secret room that contains bonus ammo and an extra life.
- Power Armor Reference: In the Cavern of Eternal Fire, players can find a power armor suit that closely resembles the original DOOM Slayer's armor, though it's not fully functional.

Activating it will trigger a cutscene that references the DOOM universe and the Doom Slayer's legacy.

### 9.3.2 Fun Easter Eggs

- DOOMguy's Lunchbox: Hidden in the Castle of Ghorath, you can find a lunchbox on a shelf with the label "DOOMguy's Lunch." If you open it, you'll receive a humorous message from DOOMguy himself, as well as a health boost.
- Doom Slayer's Music Disc: In the Necropolis of Norn, you'll find a music disc hidden in a locker, a tribute to the DOOM Slayer's heavy metal soundtrack. Playing the disc will trigger an epic rock track reminiscent of the original DOOM music, and for a limited time, you'll receive an attack speed boost.
- Cacodemon Plush: In the Wicked Caverns, there's a Cacodemon plush sitting on a shelf. Interacting with it will briefly trigger a Cacodemon laugh, and you may receive a special power-up as a bonus.

### 9.3.3 Developer References

- The Developer's Lair: Hidden deep within the Lost Halls, there's a secret room that references the developers of DOOM: The Dark Ages. It contains artwork, concept designs, and even some developer names etched into the walls as a fun tribute to those who created the game.
- "Doomsday Clock": In one of the hidden rooms in the Doomsworn Fortress, you'll find a clock stuck at midnight—a nod to the doomsday theme that has persisted throughout the entire DOOM franchise. If you interact with the clock, you'll be given a time-limited bonus.

# CHAPTER 10: TROUBLESHOOTING & FREQUENTLY ASKED QUESTIONS

## 10.1 Common Issues and Solutions

Even the most optimized games can have occasional issues. Here are some of the most common problems players face in DOOM: The Dark Ages and how to resolve them:

### 10.1.1 Game Won't Launch or Crashes on Startup

Solution:

- Check System Requirements: Ensure your PC meets the minimum or recommended system specs.
- Update Graphics Drivers: Outdated drivers are a leading cause of startup issues.
- Verify Game Files: On platforms like Steam or Epic Games, use the "Verify Integrity of Game Files" option.
- Disable Overlays: Third-party overlays (e.g., Discord, Nvidia GeForce Experience) can interfere with startup—try disabling them.

### 10.1.2 Performance Drops / FPS Stuttering

Solution:

- Lower Graphics Settings: Reduce textures, shadows, and anti-aliasing.
- Enable V-Sync or Cap FPS: Prevents GPU overrun and smooths gameplay.
- Close Background Apps: Free up system memory and CPU usage.
- Use Performance Mode (if available): Some game versions include a "Performance Mode" in settings for smoother play.

### 10.1.3 Audio Not Working or Desynced

Solution:

- Check Audio Output: Make sure your game is routed to the correct speaker or headset in system sound settings.
- Update Audio Drivers.
- Toggle Sound Settings: Switching between stereo and surround in-game sometimes corrects output issues.

### 10.1.4 Save File Corruption or Progress Lost

Solution:

- Enable Cloud Saves (if available): Cloud backups can restore lost progress.
- Back Up Save Files Manually: Save data is typically located in your system's user folder (e.g., Documents\DOOM_DarkAges\Saves).
- Avoid Interrupting Saves: Don't close the game during auto-saves.

## 10.2 In-game Glitches and Fixes

Here are a few known glitches and how to address or avoid them:

### 10.2.1 Character Getting Stuck in Geometry

Fix:

- Try jumping or dashing repeatedly.
- If stuck, pause and use Fast Travel (if unlocked).
- If all else fails, reload the last checkpoint.

### 10.2.2 Enemies Not Spawning or Stuck in Place

Fix:

- Move to another area and return—this can reset the spawn trigger.
- Restart the mission from the last checkpoint.
- Avoid skipping scripted events too quickly.

### 10.2.3 Weapon Upgrade Menu Freezes

Fix:

- This occurs most often when upgrading too quickly. Wait a second between upgrades.
- If frozen, open the pause menu and return to the upgrade screen, or reload the level.

### 10.2.4 Multiplayer Desync or Rubberbanding

Fix:

- Check your internet connection—consider using a wired connection for stability.
- Restart your router or change server region in multiplayer settings.
- Close bandwidth-heavy apps during gameplay (e.g., streaming, large downloads).

## 10.3 How to Get Help from the Community

If you've exhausted the above options, the DOOM: The Dark Ages community is an excellent resource for tips, fixes, and player-to-player support.

### 10.3.1 Official Forums and Social Channels

- Bethesda Forums: Regularly monitored by moderators and developers.
- r/DOOM on Reddit: A highly active community of fans and troubleshooters.
- Twitter/X (@DOOM): Official updates, patch notes, and responses from the dev team.
- Discord Servers: Many DOOM-related Discord communities exist with dedicated help channels.

### 10.3.2 Bug Reporting

To report bugs:

- Use the in-game feedback option (if available).
- Submit a report through the official Bethesda support page.
- Include relevant info: system specs, bug description, reproduction steps, and screenshots if possible.

### 10.3.3 Troubleshooting Resources

- YouTube Walkthroughs: Useful for visual fixes or navigating through bugged areas.
- Steam Guides: Community-created fix guides for specific hardware or unusual glitches.
- Modding Communities: Some fan-made mods patch bugs unofficially (note: use at your own risk).

# CONCLUSION

## 11.1 Final Thoughts on DOOM: The Dark Ages

DOOM: The Dark Ages takes the legendary brutality and adrenaline-fueled combat the franchise is known for and reimagines it within a grim, medieval fantasy world. From its heavy, rune-etched weapons to cursed cathedrals and demonic battlegrounds, it offers an experience both familiar and refreshingly unique.

This installment leans hard into lore, atmosphere, and intricate level design, while still delivering on core DOOM principles: fast, fluid combat, skill-based progression, and an unapologetic power fantasy. Whether you're charging into a horde with a flaming greatsword or blasting through the undead with a rune-powered shotgun, every moment is crafted to make you feel like the apex predator of hell.

But above all else, DOOM: The Dark Ages is a game of mastery—of timing, precision, aggression, and understanding the battlefield. The game doesn't just challenge you to survive—it dares you to dominate.

## 11.2 How to Become a Master Slayer

Becoming a true Slayer isn't just about unlocking all the weapons or beating the campaign—it's about mastering every mechanic, exploiting every enemy weakness, and turning the tide of battle with confidence and brutal efficiency. Here are your final steps on the path to mastery:

- Master the Combat Loop: Learn when to switch weapons, when to go melee, and how to flow from kill to kill with momentum. Always be moving, always be killing.
- Learn Enemy Patterns: Memorize tells and behaviors. The more you know, the less you bleed.

- ⚔️ Experiment with Builds: Use upgrades, weapon mods, and power-ups creatively. The best Slayers adapt.
- Know Your Environment: Every arena is designed to be used. Look for jump pads, cover, traps, and secret vantage points.
- Push the Difficulty: Playing on higher settings forces better habits. Don't fear Ultra-Violence — embrace it.
- 🔍 Explore Everything: Master Slayers find every secret, every weapon, every upgrade. Exploration is power.

Above all, remember: The Doom Slayer isn't a hero because he wins — he's a hero because he never stops.

So pick up your sword, load your cannon, and let hell tremble in your wake.

Rip and tear... until it is done.

# EXTRAS

## 12.1 Game Terms Glossary

Below is a curated list of key in-game achievements and how to unlock them. (Note: actual achievement names may vary depending on platform.)

| Achievement | Description |
|---|---|
| Welcome to the Dark Ages | Complete the prologue/tutorial. |
| First Blood | Perform your first Glory Kill. |
| Weapon Collector | Find and equip all base weapons. |
| Secrets of the Slayer | Discover 25 hidden secrets across any levels. |
| Demon Hunter | Kill 1,000 demons across all playthroughs. |
| Rune Master | Unlock all rune slots and equip a full set. |
| Doom Architect | Complete a user-made custom map (if modding is enabled). |
| The Unbroken Oath | Complete the campaign on Nightmare difficulty. |
| Overkill | Kill 5 enemies with a single shot using a fully upgraded weapon. |
| Stylish Executioner | Perform all unique Glory Kills on every enemy type. |
| Historian of Hell | Collect every lore entry and Codex page. |
| Eternal Flame | Complete all side missions and optional boss battles. |
| Slayer Supreme | 100% complete the campaign on Ultra-Nightmare (no deaths). |

## 12.2 Achievement List

Below is a curated list of key in-game achievements and how to unlock them. (Note: actual achievement names may vary depending on platform.)

| Achievement | Description |
|---|---|
| Welcome to the Dark Ages | Complete the prologue/tutorial. |
| First Blood | Perform your first Glory Kill. |
| Weapon Collector | Find and equip all base weapons. |
| Secrets of the Slayer | Discover 25 hidden secrets across any levels. |
| Demon Hunter | Kill 1,000 demons across all playthroughs. |
| Rune Master | Unlock all rune slots and equip a full set. |
| Doom Architect | Complete a user-made custom map (if modding is enabled). |
| The Unbroken Oath | Complete the campaign on Nightmare difficulty. |
| Overkill | Kill 5 enemies with a single shot using a fully upgraded weapon. |
| Stylish Executioner | Perform all unique Glory Kills on every enemy type. |
| Historian of Hell | Collect every lore entry and Codex page. |
| Eternal Flame | Complete all side missions and optional boss battles. |
| Slayer Supreme | 100% complete the campaign on Ultra-Nightmare (no deaths). |

# 12.3 Modding and Customizing the Game

While modding support varies by platform, DOOM: The Dark Ages (like past entries) encourages community creativity. Here's how you can expand and personalize your gameplay:

*12.3.1 Modding Tools (PC Only)*

- Official Mod Kit: Bethesda typically releases a set of tools for custom content. Look for updates on their website or community forums.
- Supported File Types: Mods may include maps, weapon rebalances, enemy AI tweaks, visual overhauls, and total conversions.
- Install Method: Mods are usually installed into the "Mods" or "Custom" folder in the game directory. Some may require a mod loader or manager.

*12.3.2 Types of Mods*

- Visual Mods: HD textures, lighting enhancements, UI reskins.
- Map Packs: New campaigns, arenas, or puzzle challenges created by fans.
- Weapon Mods: Add new weapons or rebalance existing ones for different playstyles.
- Enemy Packs: Introduce custom enemy types or increase spawn difficulty.
- Gameplay Tweaks: Faster movement, double-jump, infinite ammo, etc.

*12.3.3 Community Resources*

- Nexus Mods — A top site for high-quality DOOM mod downloads.
- ModDB — For major overhauls and full conversions.

- Steam Workshop (if supported) — Easy-to-install mods with active ratings and updates.
- Discord + Reddit — DOOM modding communities offer help, beta access, and collaboration opportunities.

Note: Always back up save files before installing mods, and read mod descriptions to ensure compatibility with your game version.